Addicted to Profit

Addicted to Profit

Reclaiming Our Lives from the Free Market

STUART SIM

EDINBURGH
University Press

Edinburgh University Press Ltd
22 George Square, Edinburgh

www.euppublishing.com

Typeset in 10.5/13 Palatino
by Servis Filmsetting Ltd, Stockport, Cheshire,
and printed and bound in Great Britain by
CPI Group (UK) Ltd, Croydon, CR0 4YY

A CIP record for this book is available from the British Library

ISBN 978 0 7486 4671 5 (hardback)
ISBN 978 0 7486 4672 2 (webready PDF)
ISBN 978 0 7486 5459 8 (epub)
ISBN 978 0 7486 5458 1 (Amazon ebook)

Contents

Acknowledgements   vii

 1 Introduction: It's All About Profit   1
 2 The Tyranny of Profit: Confronting an Addiction and a
    Fetish   7
 3 'What Shall It Profit a Man?': Profitless Activities   33
 4 Life Before Profit, Life Minus Profit   43
 5 Profit in the Genes?   56
 6 Neoliberalism, Financial Crisis, and Profit   70
 7 Global Warming and Profit   96
 8 Healthcare and Profit   109
 9 Education and Profit: The World of Pay-as-You-Learn   126
10 The Arts, the Media Industries, and Profit   143
11 Conclusion: It Needn't All Be About Profit   155

Notes   168
Bibliography   185
Index   195

Acknowledgements

Once again my thanks go to everyone at Edinburgh University Press, and most particularly my editor Jackie Jones, for their unfailing support and encouragement over the course of this project. It has been a pleasure to work with the Press for so many years now. Professor W. R. Owens made many helpful suggestions about the manuscript which were gratefully taken up. Doctor Helene Brandon heard the arguments being worked out, and as usual offered sound advice, especially on the topic of health debates.

1
Introduction: It's All About Profit

In the MacTaggart Lecture at the Edinburgh International Television Festival in 2009 the media tycoon James Murdoch delivered a devastating attack on the BBC, and by implication public services in general, arguing that '[t]here is an inescapable conclusion that we must reach if we are to have a better society. The only reliable, durable, and perpetual guarantor of independence is profit.'[1] Murdoch was specifically referring to press freedom here, but it is a view neatly summing up an entire lifestyle that goes under various names: neoliberalism, market fundamentalism, globalisation, or to bring out its more negative side, 'casino' or 'no-rules capitalism'.[2] Murdoch is not an economist of course, nor a professional psychologist or sociologist, but he is a particularly powerful media tycoon. The Murdoch family owns News International with its diverse and prestigious portfolio of newspapers and television networks, and such views take on considerable importance for that very reason. If people in Murdoch's position are emphasising the role of profit in human affairs then so are their many media outlets, and that has a far-reaching effect on the public consciousness, encouraging us to believe that the pursuit of profit through free-market capitalism is our destiny as a species. The message is that it is our democratic duty to support that economic system to the hilt. While it is one thing for businesses to make a profit that is reinvested in their activities and serves some public use, it is another

1

for corporations to see their sole objective as to profiteer on behalf of their shareholders. We might better call the society we live in a profitocracy than a democracy; one ruthlessly dedicated to the production of profit at the expense of the public good, and to the cult of corporate profiteering.

The dismissive tone Murdoch adopts towards public service can only be depressing to anyone who thinks there is more to life than its economic aspect, and in its vision of society as primarily a means for generating profit for *homo economicus*: that we cannot really trust anyone, or any institution, that is not concerned to make a profit out of their activities – in the public sector no less than the private. Yet tacitly or otherwise we go along with this notion in our everyday affairs, where the profit motive now dominates in so many areas, even in those in which its impact is at best highly suspect, perhaps even counterproductive: healthcare and education, for example, neither of which would seem to be all that well suited to the application of such a regimen. Neither is it healthy to treat the arts as an area which can only justify its activities if it generates financial profit, as if that were to be considered 'the only reliable, durable, and perpetual guarantor' of aesthetic value too. The aim of this book is to challenge the underlying ideology involved and its reductive view of human existence that leads us to this cultural impasse, by questioning its basic principles: is profit the reason people fall in love, have families, create art, found religions, develop their talents and abilities, vote, show compassion towards others, try to build a socially more just society? Must we live perpetually under the tyranny of profit, with its narrow-minded assumption that economic self-interest lies at the core of our being, or can a case be made for the encouragement of an anti-profit mentality that actively resists its encroachment in the name of asserting our humanity? Ultimately, I am arguing for a paradigm shift, away from our obsession with profit to a world far more concerned with social justice than the one we are living in at present seems to be.

Profit has been fetishised by our culture to the extent that views like Murdoch's can attract little adverse notice; a culture where Prime Minister David Cameron can find it quite unexceptional also to campaign for action against the threat posed by global warming on the grounds that there are potentially huge profits to be made by those willing to invest in developing green technology: 'I passionately believe that by recasting the argument for action on climate change away from the language of threats and punishments and into positive, profit-making terms, we can have a much wider impact.'[3] He is not alone in making this observation: it was emphasised in the highly influential Stern report of 2007 as well, although obviously it takes on more weight when voiced by such a high-profile public figure as a government leader of a major Western nation.[4] But it carries the implication that if profit were not forthcoming then the exercise would not be worth bothering about, certainly not an issue for the business sector to concern itself with anyway. When we look at the impact of the profit motive on areas such as healthcare, education, and the arts, however, its detrimental effect soon becomes abundantly apparent: never mind the disasters that can unfold in areas where profit is the acknowledged objective, such as banking and the finance industry in general. There are lessons to be learned from this obsession and they would benefit from being brought more fully into open public debate, because the political ethos of the times, despite the continuing reverberations of the financial crisis of 2007–8 several years later when even America's creditworthiness is now being called into question by credit agencies, is to keep pushing further on down this road regardless and in the process to make human affairs progressively more subject to the profit motive.[5] Neoliberals cannot bring themselves to give up their commitment to this, no matter what evidence may accumulate of its detrimental effect on human relations and our general quality of life.

I will be arguing against that ideologically driven project and suggesting that we can develop an anti-profit mentality to offset its baleful effect: that we are capable of being more than a self-interested *homo economicus* with a one-dimensional view of existence focused on financial gain. The structure of this book, which is intended to be both a critical study and a manifesto for cultural change, is as follows: after establishing the nature and socio-cultural ramifications of the problem, Chapter 2, 'The Tyranny of Profit', will go on to outline what an anti-profit mentality taking issue with profit and profiteering could involve. I will be suggesting a series of ways we might develop such a mentality, by means of changes in our lifestyle and beliefs at the level of the individual as well as by engaging in various kinds of collective direct action and public campaigns to protect our threatened social institutions. Inspiration will be drawn from such sources as Gilles Deleuze and Félix Guattari's now-famous attack on social conformity, *Anti-Oedipus* (1972), in order to set up 'Profit' as the new demon, or 'addiction' as I perceive it, to be resisted;[6] and also from Slavoj Žižek's concept of the fetish, which goes a long way towards explaining the psychology at work behind our apparent complicity with the forces of 'Profit'.[7] Chapter 3, 'What Shall It Profit a Man?', surveys those human activities on which profit apparently has no bearing. Compassionate behaviour is not profit-driven, as a case in point, and neither is spirituality; nor, in a general sense, is the creative impulse. Chapter 4, 'Life Before Profit, Life Minus Profit', moves on to look at how societies operated in pre-capitalist times when profit was not fetishised as it is nowadays, to ask whether there is anything we can still learn from them in this respect, while making it clear that this is not designed as a campaign for a return to a pre-modern lifestyle – such as some of the more radical elements in the Green movement have been known to recommend, as if they quite relish the prospect of turning their back on technology and industrialisation. It will also look at various movements in recent times which have set up systems in which profit played no part, 'life minus profit'. Communism is an outstanding example of such a system, but there is also Islamic culture to consider, since on theological grounds it forbids interest on loans, leading to very different banking practices from which the West might well learn. Chapter 5, 'Profit in the Genes?', will assess the scientific and sociological arguments for altruism and selfish individualism respectively, to see what grounds there may be for choosing to base one's social structure on one or the other trait. Is there conclusive evidence of us being hard-wired one way or the other to be cooperative or competitive? And if not, what then? The implications of the current 'Social Brain' project will be considered in some detail here. Chapters 6 through 10 examine the impact, in the main highly detrimental I shall be contending, of the profit motive in various key areas of our lives: from the role it has played in the credit crisis and global warming (Chapters 6 and 7), to its insidious infiltration into healthcare provision, higher education, and the world of the arts (Chapters 8, 9, and 10 respectively). The distorting effect of neoliberal economics on human affairs will be emphasised throughout this section, and its many internal contradictions foregrounded. Here we have an ideology based on the premise of the innate rationality of the market, when in reality the market provokes some of the most irrational behaviour imaginable that can wreck the carefully worked-out plans of both individuals and entire nations, sometimes overnight. The market may be rational in responding adversely to the unsustainable debts run up by countries like Iceland, Ireland, and Greece, but those debts could not have built up in the first place without market investment and market collusion. Chapter 11 concludes by recommending that, in the short term, we shift our focus culturally from living for the sake of creating profit to living *with* it; then in the longer term, that we strive to create a society where the profit ideology is comprehensively de-fetishised and we can consider ourselves free from the shackles of neoliberal economics. There is both a reformist and a radical perspective to this: reformists will call for greater emphasis to be put on wealth distribution than wealth generation; radicals for a lifestyle in which other aspects of our nature are given precedence over the entrepreneurial, and society is geared towards helping us to develop these. The value of each position will be assessed, but the critical point is that as far as both are concerned, it *needn't* all be about profit.

Overall, the narrative arc of the book runs from articulating the problem and some projected solutions to it, through detailing profit's negative effect on our lives and then on to considering how best to approach dealing with it tactically so that we can move towards anti-profit as a social ideal, rather than allowing the ideology of the likes of James Murdoch to be given free rein. Or to put it more succinctly: what we could be doing to cure our addiction, why we ought to be doing it, and how to set about achieving it. The project is to be seen as extending and elaborating on the arguments put forward in my recent books *The Carbon Footprint Wars: What Might Happen If We Retreat From Globalization?* and *The End of Modernity: What the Financial and Environmental Crisis Is Really Telling Us*, where I questioned the sustainability of our current socio-economic system.[8] *Addicted to Profit* delves yet more deeply into the driving force behind that system, to form a more comprehensive critique of our current cultural set-up. At one time profit was put forward as the route to a better life, the way to improve the conditions of human existence for all. Now, however, courtesy of the hegemony of neoliberalism, profit has been turned into the whole reason for our existence, as if this was the point of our evolution as a species, and that is just dehumanising. As far as the Murdoch doctrine is concerned, it's all about profit: I want to contest that judgement.

2

The Tyranny of Profit: Confronting an Addiction and a Fetish

The profit motive has been applied to more and more areas of our lives by our political classes, such that the 'business model' has become the major criterion by which almost all public services are judged; judged, and then all too often found badly wanting by those same classes, and thus candidates for wholesale reconstruction. Privatisation is consistently held up as the solution to all our public service needs, and public utilities such as water and electricity are systematically being hived off from the public sector internationally. It would have to be said, however, that the latter exercise has led to very mixed results in terms of both efficiency and cost to the consumer. On this score, a recent auditing report has criticised the UK Border Patrol for concentrating on profit-making activities at the expense of its core duties.[1] Even the armed forces have not been immune from this imperative, with the Halliburton company winning some extremely lucrative contracts to take over many of the services of the American military in Iraq in recent years; a situation which raises complex ethical issues. Even though Halliburton eventually fell foul of the American government for systematic overcharging of its services, that was felt to be an indictment of the company itself rather than the policy of outsourcing as such. Although mercenary soldiers can still figure prominently in conflicts in Africa, their use has generally been phased out amongst Western nations. Any change to that policy could have some very profound implications on our public life. Whether we could rely on mercenary armies the way we do on native-born ones is only one of a host of questions that comes to mind in this context, and it would have to be said that the notion of killing others for personal profit is particularly abhorrent.

The necessity for profit-creation now exercises an effective tyranny over the public sphere, no area of this seeming immune from its influence, and it is increasingly intruding into the private as well. Education and self-development, for example, are currently being encouraged mainly on the basis that they can improve one's earning power; hence the Murdoch doctrine: the more profit you can show from your activities, then the more free you are assumed to be as an individual. Murdoch's MacTaggart speech will be analysed in more detail later in this chapter to challenge what I will argue are its highly spurious underlying assumptions. Profit from this standpoint guarantees you independence, an emotive argument in a society like ours with its cult of individualism. Profit, I am going to argue instead however, drawing on the theories of Slavoj Žižek, has become fetishised by almost all of us.[2] Even socialist-inclined governments throughout the West think primarily in its terms of reference these days, having largely given up the idea of engineering any truly fundamental change in the system and contenting themselves with instigating minor reforms to it instead. This activity alone is enough to bring down on them the ire of the neoliberal lobby, since neoliberals want no tinkering with the market at all.

David Harvey's definition of neoliberalism makes very clear what this doctrine commits us to collectively:

> Neoliberalism is in the first instance a theory of political economic practices that proposes that human well-being can best be advanced by liberating individual entrepreneurial freedoms and skills within an institutional framework characterized by strong private property rights, free markets, and free trade. The role of the state is to create and preserve an institutional framework appropriate to such practices. The state has to guarantee, for example, the quality and integrity of money.

It must also set up those military, defence, police, and legal structures
and functions required to secure private property rights and to guarantee, by force if need be, the proper functioning of markets.[3]

Harvey goes on to note that the state also considers itself as being
under an obligation to create markets in areas which previously
were thought to be best kept under public control: 'land, water,
education, health care, social security, or environmental pollution'.[4]
Everything and anything, it would appear, is henceforth to be considered available and acceptable for trading on the open market.
In consequence, we are expected to adopt a much more market-
oriented view of social existence. The state becomes the servant of
the market, which is taken to be above mere politics.

The assumption made by neoliberals is that the more profit that is
generated in a society then the more of it will filter down the social
chain, leading to improved living standards for us all – eventually
anyway. Pragmatism is to the fore in such cases, with the system's
(assumed) beneficial effects being taken to excuse any accommodation that has to be made with it ideologically. Leftist politicians in
the West have long since made their peace with capitalist economics; in the immortal words of the Labour politician Peter Mandelson
after his party's election victory in 1997, the left is now 'intensely
relaxed' about the rich becoming ever richer, and no longer feels
the need to rein them in.[5] That this is a development for the overall
public good is now all but an article of faith amongst Western
politicians, few of whom will ever venture publicly to challenge the
hegemony that has been established by neoliberalism lest this scare
away international investors, who in an age of globalisation will
simply shop around for more congenial national markets.

Marxist and far-left theorists have observed this development
with growing frustration, since it does not fit in with their view of
how capitalism should create more, not less, opposition amongst
the general public over the years. Neoliberalism should work to the
advantage of such theories, but to date it has not and that invites
some more imaginative speculation as to why. The following
example offers a very different take on history that, questionable

though it is in various respects, might nevertheless cast new light on the problem. Jean-François Lyotard made many enemies on the left when he suggested that the working classes in nineteenth-century Britain were swept up in the excitement of industrialisation and the unprecedented changes it was bringing about in national life, rather than being the oppressed and exploited mass of Marxist legend:

> [T]he English unemployed did not become workers to survive, they [. . .] *enjoyed* the hysterical, masochistic, whatever exhaustion it was of *hanging on* in the mines, in the foundries, in the factories, in hell, they enjoyed it, enjoyed the mad destruction of their organic body which was indeed imposed on them, they enjoyed the decomposition of their personal identity, the identity that the peasant tradition had constructed for them, enjoyed the dissolution of their families and villages[.][6]

Having turned into something of a lapsed Marxist by the time he wrote this in the 1970s, Lyotard was deliberately trying to provoke the left in this instance by mocking one of its most cherished beliefs in the alienation of labour in the modern world, leading to an undercurrent of dissent in society at large. In retrospect, however, what he was describing was an addiction, and it is an addiction which has persisted through to our own day and the establishment of the empire of neoliberalism.

The depth of the addiction means that that we have something of a consensus as to macro-economic policy across the West, therefore, with profit right at the very centre. In a sense, we are all neoliberals now, even if only passively.

One particular example of how much against the public interest it can be to surrender public control of national resources to the market can be found in the case of the privatisation of the Bolivian water industry in 1999. This was an event forced on the government by pressure from the IMF and the World Bank in return for loans to stabilise the economy, which was struggling against inflation. Upon privatisation, water rates were suddenly increased by as much as 100–200 per cent, meaning that water use was eating up as much as 20 per cent of the average monthly wage in an already desperately poor country by Western standards. When riots broke out over this in the city of Cochabamba, these were put down by government troops at considerable loss of life, drawing international condemnation. The government ultimately relented and in 2001 re-nationalised the industry, but soon found itself being sued by one of the aggrieved privatisers, the multinational Bechtel Corporation, for lost future profits. This was merely one of a string of what the Public Citizen website has reported as 'water privatization fiascos' around the globe.[7] To these can be added various electricity, gas, and public transport fiascos too, almost always undertaken in the cause of cutting public spending, and all too often at the behest of the IMF and World Bank.

Neoliberalism represents a particularly purist interpretation of laissez-faire economics, so it is not in itself new in its drive to make this a world fit for market trading: the capitalists of Marx's time would recognise it immediately, and be entirely sympathetic to its goals. Yet the extent to which this ethos becomes an end in itself rather than a means to improve the human lot is rarely addressed. As I put it earlier, we have fetishised the concept of profit, and effectively bracketed any qualms we may have had about this cultural shift. While there are some on the far left who still speak out against economic exploitation, both in the West and in the developing countries, and the increasing disparity between the income levels and wealth of those at the top and bottom in Western society in general, the political mainstream has long since turned a blind eye to them and they have next to no effect on public policy. My concern will now be how we can counteract this phenomenon, using campaigning of various kinds at both local and national levels, strategic use of civil disobedience and non-cooperation with the authorities, as well as continued efforts through all the media that are available to us to raise public consciousness of how profit has come to distort our lives and led to the loss of key public institutions to exacerbate this trend.

'Fetishisation' and 'Making the Best of It'

Žižek's concept of fetishisation captures the working of a very human trait, which could be described in colloquial terms as

11

'making the best of it': if you find yourself unable to do anything much about your surroundings, political as well as physical, then you will just have to learn to adapt to them somehow or other. Jean-Paul Sartre had pointed out earlier in the twentieth century that we are for much of the time in our lives in situations we did not create ourselves, or may actively dislike and wish would go away, but we are nevertheless free to choose how we respond to them.[8] Choice was right at the heart of the existentialist project, and as long as we could exercise it, no matter how limited the options available to us actually were, then we could be said to be free and to have some measure of control over our destiny. Sartre was writing in the dark days of the Second World War when France was under German occupation and the choice on offer often reduced itself to something quite stark: cooperate with the occupying forces or defy them and put your life in danger. Those who joined the Resistance movement chose the latter route; whereas some others entered into enthusiastic collaboration with their conquerors, gaining numerous personal privileges by doing so. Most of the population, however, even if they hated living under tyranny, kept their heads down and got on with their lives as best as they could under the trying circumstances that were the order of the day; even if, as the historian H. R. Kedward has noted, this took the form of 'sullen resentment' or '"attentisme", a waiting on events and doing nothing of any substance in any direction'.[9] Not everyone is a hero, nor should we expect them to be when tyranny of this kind comes on the scene, much as we might applaud those with the courage to be so.

Žižek's point is more subtle. He is describing what happens once tyranny becomes the normal state of affairs and there is no apparent prospect of it being overturned; nor even a readily available channel through which to express opposition that might eventually effect change in the system. All such options seem to be closed off. What happens then is that the opposition is internalised, and not just that, but hidden away under apparent support for the tyranny. As Žižek puts it, we both know and don't know simultaneously that the regime is not in our best interests and that its actions cannot be justified: 'one knows the falsehood very well, one is well aware of a particular interest hidden behind an ideological universality, but still one does not renounce it.'[10] Making the best of it under those conditions means that we manage to convince ourselves that the regime is nevertheless worth following and that we accept its values, while knowing somewhere deep down within ourselves that this is in effect a lie, that we do not really believe it. This is the state of mind that Žižek refers to as 'enlightened false consciousness'.[11] Peter Sloterdijk, whose work influenced Žižek on the subject of ideology, puts this somewhat more provocatively as an example of 'cynical reason' on the individual's part.[12] In Žižek's view it was the widespread incidence of enlightened false consciousness that enabled the communist regimes of Eastern Europe to survive as long as they did, their many social and economic failings over the years notwithstanding.[13] No doubt if Nazi Germany had won the war then most of the population of the defeated countries, out of sheer psychological necessity as much as anything, would have come to a similar accommodation, no matter how grudging it may have been, with those in power.

In one sense enlightened false consciousness could be considered a gesture of defeat, since you are conceding that the regime under which you are living cannot be overturned and to all intents and purposes is here to stay; in which case your own insignificance becomes painfully obvious. But looked at in another way it is a positive decision to take; a rejection of the role of the downtrodden individual, a sincere attempt to give the prevailing ideology the benefit of the doubt and to embrace its ideals – although that is not intended to be an endorsement of the response, as it isn't in Žižek either. The accommodation cannot be depended upon indefinitely by those in power, and as we know, the communist regimes in Europe eventually did come to an end; but the critical point is that almost any system, whether openly tyrannical or not, can inspire such a reaction. After a certain point it informs our personal life history to such an extent that we feel the need to uphold it and to go on believing in its values. We feel the need to 'enjoy' our 'symptom' as Žižek provokingly puts it, much as Lyotard was suggesting the

English working class 'enjoyed' rampant industrialisation perhaps, with the symptom and the fetish in an interesting state of tension:

> Fetish is a kind of *envers* of the symptom. That is to say, symptom is the exception which disturbs the surface of false appearance, the point at which the repressed Other Scene erupts, while fetish is the embodiment of the lie which enables us to sustain the unbearable truth. Let us take the death of a beloved person: in the case of a symptom, I 'repress' this death, I try not to think about it, but the repressed trauma returns in the symptom; in the case of a fetish, on the contrary, I 'rationally' fully accept this death, and yet I cling to the fetish, to some feature that embodies for me the disavowal of this death.[14]

Thus the symptom keeps reminding us what is the case, but the fetish keeps refusing to acknowledge what is the case: we both know and don't know.

It is, as I put it earlier, a very human trait to react in this manner: as Žižek describes it, we are being 'realists' when we behave like this, especially if what we are facing is indeed an 'unbearable truth' or a 'miserable reality' like living under a totalitarian political regime.[15] It is also a fair assessment to make that we are doing so as I write in the aftermath of the credit crisis, a 'miserable reality' if ever there was one: that is, going along with what is deemed to be necessary in order to rehabilitate the profit ethos that we have all grown up under, and have reached the stage that we can hardly envisage life without any more. We are at least in part responsible for the tyranny that profit has come to exercise over our lives, and it will not go away unless we change our attitude to it – and quite radically too. That is what this study overall is designed to encourage.

Profiling the Tyranny of Profit

Where do we come across the tyranny of profit these days, and what kind of profile does it have? It is there in the business world certainly, and that is only to be expected in an activity where profit is almost the sole *raison d'être*, but also in a wide range of less expected areas that at one time were thought to be safe from its pernicious influence – education and health most notably. In higher education profit has now become the new criterion of value, overshadowing such phenomena as the desire for self-development or the wish to make oneself useful to society through the dissemination of one's knowledge to others. One is now encouraged to regard higher education primarily as a route to higher lifetime earnings; so the idea is that one no longer goes to an institution of higher education to develop one's latent talents or broaden one's mind, but to invest in one's economic future. It has all become very narrowly personal: money spent now will guarantee a higher return later, and as it is your money you have every incentive to focus yourself on that goal above all other considerations. Knowledge equals hard cash, and even postgraduate work has been infiltrated by this ethos: Master's and doctoral work can be calculated to add x amount to your lifetime earnings on top of a bachelor's degree, so they are worth considering – on that basis alone it would seem.

At this point it would be useful to go into the details of James Murdoch's MacTaggart Lecture, with its ringing endorsement of the profit ethic as an integral part of the democratic lifestyle. This is a sentiment straight out of the school of Milton Friedman, collectively the architects of neoliberalism's recent rise to pre-eminence. Murdoch's specific target is British official broadcasting policy, although its arguments can be made to apply to almost any area of business. The problem with the policy in place, for Murdoch, is that it is based on central planning, with the government laying down rules as to who can broadcast and what they can and cannot do once granted a licence. As Murdoch sees it this is a repressive system, and '[t]he result is lost opportunities for enterprise, free choice and commercial investment.'[16] The worst villain of the piece is the BBC, which is funded by public money and thus has no need to compete on the open market with its rivals: its survival is apparently assured no matter what it does or what its audience share happens to be. It has grown so big on this public subsidy that it has swamped all its potential rivals, such as Murdoch's Sky TV network which has no guaranteed income stream to fall back upon and must instead compete with other commercial broadcasters for advertisers' money

– which in its turn is dependent on the size of the audience it is able to attract. These are problems that the BBC never has to face, it has an unfair advantage in that its income stream is guaranteed; although it does have to negotiate this with each government, and high viewing figures obviously give its arguments more weight at the bargaining table. What is at risk under the current system, Murdoch contends, is 'the provision of independent news, investment in professional journalism, and the innovation and growth of creative industries', and without these the public suffers, as indeed does the very concept of democracy.[17]

Murdoch works hard throughout his speech to promote an image of commercial broadcasting, and commercial media in general, as public-spirited, in giving the public what it wants and offering it a diversity of views that is critical to the health of a democratic society. It is a mixture of government intervention and BBC power that is preventing this diversity, this free circulation of opinion, from being as available in the UK as it should be, and Murdoch wants it to be removed – for the greater public good as he conceives of it. Competition is an absolutely necessary element of democratic life for someone of Murdoch's outlook, and in pretty well any sphere of it that you care to name: for the historian Niall Ferguson it is also one of the critical factors that has led to global domination by Western civilisation, in which case the profit motive takes centre stage in the development of modern history.[18] No doubt the model in the back of Murdoch's mind is the American broadcasting system, where there is no significant publicly funded network on the BBC scale. The National Public Radio (NPR) there is a small operation and very poorly resourced by European standards, and it presents little threat to outfits like Murdoch's Fox Channel, with its infamous far right-wing news programmes.[19] 'If we are to have that state sponsorship at all', he insists, 'then it is fundamental to the health of the creative industries, independent production, and professional journalism that it exists on a far, far smaller scale.'[20] The argument is that when such a condition is brought about, with the BBC reduced to something like the status of the NPR perhaps, then we shall all be more independent, more in control of our destiny in having more opinions to listen to and ponder on, more choice to exercise. As far as Murdoch is concerned, only profit can guarantee this state of affairs.

Even if one accepted that Murdoch really was more interested in protecting our democratic freedoms than in the pursuit of profit for its own sake – a big 'if' I would suggest, as it must be with any major business tycoon – his argument still falls down on several counts. Diversity is not always what you end up with when advertising revenue is the main source of funding for media companies: advertisers are notoriously conservative in their views, and generally prefer to deal with companies that appeal to the popular market without causing any controversy that might affect their jealously guarded image in the public eye. This tends to encourage a convergence of style and content between all the companies targeting that market, as that is the obvious way to increase advertising revenue, and thus of course one's profit margins. Diversity from this perspective can come to mean just several versions of much the same thing, with companies unwilling to take chances that might alienate their audience in any way, leading to a fall in viewing figures and a consequent fall in advertising revenue. That market is cut-throat at the best of the times, and the aftermath of an economic crisis is plainly not the best of times, so the pattern is to play as safe as possible and produce copies, or variations, of whatever happens to be drawing large audiences at any one time. If a reality television programme proves popular, try another one, and then another – and don't stop until viewing figures fall significantly. Choice can be a rather dubious concept under such circumstances. One could argue that in real terms commercial companies have far less independence than entities like the BBC, because they are in the final analysis beholden to advertisers: the BBC does not have this kind of pressure, subtle though it may be, to worry about.

It is all too convenient for Murdoch to argue that profit is a means to a democratic end, when in real terms profit is an end in itself for organisations such as his family's media empire. Any organisation with shareholders will soon find itself being asked awkward questions if it starts pursuing wider social goals at the expense of its profit margins. The latter, as enshrined in company law, is taken to be its primary responsibility towards those shareholders, and as far as many companies are concerned it is the only responsibility they need really bother about. It is a view put with characteristic bluntness by Milton Friedman in an article entitled 'The social responsibility of business is to increase its profits', where he argued that businessmen who 'believe that they are defending free enterprise when they declaim that business is not concerned "merely" with profit but also with promoting desirable "social" ends', are in fact 'preaching pure and unadulterated socialism'.[21] It is worthy of note in this context that the Murdoch group owns the Star TV cable channel based in Hong Kong, and seems happy enough to pursue profit there without insisting that Western-style diversity and democratic freedoms are a prerequisite to its operation. Lecturing the Chinese government would only lead to the Star channel being blocked, as the Chinese government has done in many other cases, as with the Internet, so the pragmatics of profit win out instead.

When it comes to creative artists, they are likely to have more freedom to express themselves on a public channel than on one which has to be careful never to offend advertisers. Few creative artists would want their work to be broken up constantly by advertising breaks either: they will go along with this if that is the only way to get their work screened, but that is not the same thing as acceptance of the practice, which can be very irritating indeed. Much the same goes for audiences, for whom advertising is little more than a necessary evil to be received passively. The occasional ad can be diverting, but who, other than advertisers themselves or those who work for advertising agencies, ever tunes in to watch ads rather than the programmes they interrupt? It is the profit ethic that requires such interruptions not the creative aesthetic.

As you would expect, the BBC reacted strongly to Murdoch's criticisms and several of its high-profile staff leapt to its defence, spiritedly putting the case for public service broadcasting; but again, the point needs to be made that Murdoch's outlook is the dominant one in the business world and it cannot simply be discounted as an instance of professional jealousy. The vast majority of those in positions of business power sincerely do believe that '[t]he only reliable, durable, and perpetual guarantor of independence is profit', and are not really open to any arguments to the contrary. The mere existence of organisations like the BBC constitutes an affront to their ideology, and it will always be vulnerable to such sniping. It is not a matter that the Murdochs of this world can let rest: the supposed virtues of profit must be proclaimed at every opportunity, and it helps if you can give the impression of occupying the moral high ground when doing so.

The stock market represents the profit ethic taken to its extreme, and the extent of its influence on our lives has grown immensely in recent years as the search for ever greater profit margins – 'alpha', in the market traders' jargon[22] – has drawn entire countries into its orbit, making their economic survival contingent on its whims. Iceland, Ireland, and Greece are outstanding examples of the process, although others are predicted to follow. As long as the market was booming, such countries could attract investment, but when boom became bust investors found themselves staring at unsustainable debt mountains that bore little relationship to actual gross domestic product, and that could not be repaid. The result was economic chaos in each case. Every time that happens it creates ripples of anxiety throughout the rest of what is now very much an interconnected global economic system. Some influential commentators are even predicting, against the grain of the official line on this, which tends to preach confidence in the underlying economy, that growth might never return at all.[23]

In a sense, the stock market itself is a gigantic confidence trick, as no one really thinks they are going to lose when they buy stocks and shares and play the market; certainly, no one plans to lose, no matter how much the mantra that 'the worth of your stocks may go up as well as down' is repeated. So it is a confidence trick that we are all playing on ourselves, and seem content to go on doing even in the aftermath of stock market crashes. Somehow we are able to convince ourselves that each occurrence of collapse is an anomaly, rather than a sign of an underlying instability that will keep recurring, regardless of how much technological progress we may achieve in the interim: one of the more dubious examples of enlightened false consciousness around at the moment. One of the main reasons for the recent crisis is that financial institutions were willing to take huge risks on their borrowing to expand their business, on the grounds that the stock market would continue on ever upward and that today's borrowing would be rendered insignificant by tomorrow's increased profit returns. We all know where that mistaken belief has landed us.

So how can we free ourselves from such mistaken beliefs that so consistently emerge from the neoliberal fetish? Let us turn for possible inspiration to an earlier attempt at breaking the stranglehold of social conformity in which we find ourselves so persistently caught, *Anti-Oedipus*.

Anti-Oedipus: Anti-Profit?

Gilles Deleuze and Félix Guattari's *Anti-Oedipus* is one the most famous, and also, it has to be admitted, infamous, works of modern critical-cultural theory. It is a maverick exercise in recommending that, for example, schizophrenia is one possible way – indeed, the *recommended* way – to counter the power of what the authors term 'Oedipus'. Oedipus stands as a symbol for all the conformist pressures of modern Western culture that act to constrain our individuality and keep us in line: 'A schizophrenic out for a walk is a better model than a neurotic lying on the analyst's couch.'[24] The individual is urged to resist the domination of Oedipus by being as non-conformist as he or she can, employing whatever means may be needed to undermine the system that is so formidably arrayed against him or her. It is an extreme and deliberately provocative work of theorising designed to make us rethink how we should function in the face of pressures to conform socially, since such conformity is to the benefit of those in power. I intend to take a lead from this model and set up 'Profit' as the symbol for everything that forces us to accept a lifestyle almost exclusively based on economic factors, where the end result has been that we have internalised this

20

to the point that we simply accept it as the natural order of things, almost without question.

In the first instance, the more people who are saying this, writing about it, making programmes about it, and in general confronting the public with this information and challenging them to think more about their lifestyle choices, how they can express their dissatisfaction to the political parties, then the better. In the UK at the moment, the coalition government has managed to convince the electorate that the budget deficit was caused by reckless overspending by the last administration rather than the bailout of the banks that pretty well all Western governments found themselves having to mount. Even fundamentally right-wing governments like the American under the Republican leadership of President Bush felt they had to join in this rescue act, and all to the tune, as Charles Morris's book remind us, of two trillion dollars. That book's history is worth recounting to indicate the almost unimaginable scale of losses we are dealing in. It came out originally in a hardback edition entitled *The Trillion Dollar Meltdown*, but by the time the paperback was published a few months later the author felt the need to amend the title to *The Two Trillion Dollar Meltdown*, explaining that,

> [i]n the first edition of this book, I estimated the losses of the banking and other investment sectors would be at least $trillion, specifying that if the deleveraging is disorderly, the losses could be double or triple that amount. We now seem to be in the midst of a disorderly deleveraging.[25]

Perhaps we should be thankful that Morris has not yet seen the need to publish *The Three Trillion Dollar Meltdown*. The overspend argument really deserves to be challenged more persistently because it has formed the rationale for the massive public spending cuts that we are now experiencing in countries like the UK. Societies have been addicted to many unfair and anti-social activities in the past that they managed subsequently to overcome, slavery being an outstanding example, and that means persistent campaigning of the kind being recommended here.

There are clear signs coming to light around us, however, that we are growing increasingly aware of the downside of the lifestyle that

'Profit' promotes and that a sense of dissatisfaction is beginning to make itself felt – anti-globalisation campaigns, anti-capitalist movements, public protests in countries like Britain, Greece, and Ireland against swingeing public service cuts, for example. These are to be encouraged as much as possible, particularly at local level. Social networking has its role to play too in helping to organise practical protests, such as sit-ins and occupations of services about to be cut, like libraries, local hospitals, advice centres, and youth centres. Even if these activities do not prevent closures from occurring eventually, they are worth conducting to draw attention to what is happening at local level because of national government decisions, and to stir up publicity. Scope is also there to develop single-issue political groupings to contest local elections, where the monopoly of the big national parties is easier to challenge than it is in general elections. Such concerted opposition from the grass roots gains media coverage and we need more and more of that if we are to make people in general reconsider their lifestyle.

There has also been a highly symbolic campaign against bankers' bonuses in Holland, which has been so successful in rousing popular support that it has prompted the Dutch parliament to pass a law against the practice in those cases where banks have been bailed out by the public purse. The Netherlands, as one commentator has put it, 'is now vying for the title of Europe's most bonus-hating country'.[26] This is a lead well worth following, since it was only the threat of a mass withdrawal of deposits that made the banks and the politicians realise that something had to be done to placate the public. The Dutch banks have since apologised for being 'insensitive' to public opinion on this issue, whereas in the UK their counterparts are content to repeat the threat that their senior staff will move elsewhere if such a policy is ever instituted. Consumer boycotts of this kind have been under-utilised to date, and can be turned against any company that the public feels is taking advantage of it, say by excessive profit margins, or breaching workers' rights, or exploiting labour unfairly in the developing world. Many companies manifestly are engaging in such exploitation, and it is something that we in the West ought be deeply ashamed of, and more willing to take action against. Again, social networking offers a useful tool by which to mobilise action quickly on such fronts: viral campaigning is obviously going to become increasingly important in ideological struggle.

We also need to start thinking more creatively at individual, and what Jean-François Lyotard called 'little narrative' level, to build up a mass consciousness concerned to combat 'Profit':[27] to become self-consciously 'Anti-Profit' in our outlook and to do our best to get ourselves noticed so that others will be inspired to follow our example. I want to put forward some equivalents to the turn to schizophrenia in *Anti-Oedipus*, therefore, with the same provocative, and iconoclastic, intent: to make us recognise that we do not have to conform, or tacitly accept social injustice, or turn a blind eye to the inequalities in the world around us. Options exist, some easier to put into practice than others perhaps, but options nevertheless do exist.

I want to draw further inspiration from the rise of socialism, which at various points in the past, throughout Western European society, has been very influential in the political domain in changing social policy. We seem to have lost much of the fervour that socialism, taking the term in a fairly broad sense, could arouse in the public at large, with neoliberalism gradually becoming ideologically dominant. Yet if laissez-faire economics had been allowed to run completely unchecked from the nineteenth century onwards, we would most likely have a very different kind of society than we now do, with a minimum of public services, and most likely even greater disparities of wealth between the upper and lower levels of society than currently apply. Arguments have to keep being put forward about the virtues of the state, and public institutions in general, in protecting the individual from the excesses of the free market; otherwise the neoliberal policy of progressively less government will leave the majority of us horribly exposed to the whims of the market and the machinations of those with a big stake in profit. We've forgotten what socialist ideals have achieved and we should be reminded of these, and made aware of what we run the risk of losing if the neoliberal argument is allowed to win the day. If the public sector is dissolved it will be a backward step socially, and one from which most of us will suffer.

Neither is there any need to be doctrinaire about this, claiming that any one version of socialism has all the answers as to how to overcome neoliberalism. Marxism, for example, certainly gives one a set of ready-made answers as to what to do to change society, but we are all well aware by now of the drawbacks to a totally centralised society of the kind that Marxists invariably want to establish. There has to be something in between totalitarianism and the anarchy of the unregulated market, however, and at the very least an injection of socialism into the political mainstream seems to be worth campaigning for – even if this involves reviving discussion about the possibility of the construction of a 'Third Way', a topic that will be picked up in more detail in Chapter 5. We have to remember that socialist principles were introduced into Western society beforehand, and accepted by the population at large as being for the common good, as a necessary check on the excesses of the free market economy; that is why we have the various institutions of the welfare state, such as, most notably in the UK, the National Health Service. Campaigning for a return to socialist principles of this broad type strikes me as an entirely worthy exercise in which to engage.

Non-Cooperation with Profit

What might a policy of principled and systematic non-cooperation with 'Profit' look like? Here are some practical suggestions:

- For a start, we could very usefully follow the example of the Netherlands and campaign insistently for consumer boycotts when companies misbehave, especially against the banks, which for all their apparent power are nevertheless very vulnerable to such an exercise. If companies exploit developing world labour in order to produce cheap clothing, or whatever other product, then stop shopping there and publicly encourage others to do the same so that the company is forced to take notice and amend its policies. Public shaming of irresponsible business practice is an option we can all exercise.

- Campaign for banks to be turned into public utilities, like water and electricity supplies, although not to be privatised as the latter now tend to be throughout the West, since this merely encourages the owners to see how far they can push costs up, as it is clearly in their interests, and those of their shareholders, to do. The goal would be to remove the profit motive from such services and to move power away from shareholders, who can only regard the general public as a source to exploit – as we saw all too clearly in the 'fiasco' of the privatised Bolivian water industry. Eventually, what all such activities should be encouraging us to do is to stop thinking like a consumer. The point to remember is that where there are consumers someone, or some company, is benefitting financially, and that is the only reason for their involvement; there is never anything altruistic or public-spirited about it, everything else is subsidiary to the accumulation of profit. Companies and entrepreneurs care about things like democracy only inasmuch as they make it easier for them to shift their product.

- Other commentators see virtue in becoming involved in local enterprises which steer clear of profit, putting public service first in an attempt to improve our immediate environment. Douglas Rushkoff is a particular advocate of this in his provocative book *Life Inc.*, a spirited attack on the hold that corporatism has come to exert over us:

> If we can forget about the Dow Jones Industrial Average for long enough to remember who we are and what value we might truly bring to this world, we may just be able to take back the world we have ceded to a six-hundred-year-old business deal.[28]

Rushkoff has several recommendations as to how we can circumvent corporatist control and the urge to make profit, and they work mainly at a local level, making them easy to access and run. 'Small is the new big', he insists, 'and the surest path to global change in a highly networked world is to make an extremely local impact that works so well it spreads.'[29] So we are asked to engage in 'bottom-up activism', which can involve anything from promoting rooftop agriculture in urban areas, buying where we can from 'community-supported-agriculture groups' (CSAs) rather than relying on 'Big Agra' for all our fresh food, to developing local currency systems, or even 'local economic transfer systems (LETS)' whereby individuals trade complementary services with each other.[30] Small-scale though these may be, cumulatively they help to give us a new way of looking at the world in which we are participants rather than just passive consumers.

- Don't buy stocks and shares, since that only encourages the worst instincts we have: to make a quick profit without any apparent effort on our part. If you never play the stock market then at least you'll have the satisfaction of knowing that you are not one of those directly responsible for creating a stock market crash, the effect of which is to damage the whole fabric of society, not just the bank balance of investors. Panic selling played its role in bringing about the last crash, as investors responded to rumours of imminent failures, as well as falls in share prices triggered by hedge funds indulging in the sharp practice of short selling, by which even corporate collapses become a source of profit for some. If you stay away from the stock market you will never find yourself being manoeuvred into positions where you have to make such decisions. Investment of all kinds by individuals probably has to be considered suspect, since it is rarely going to be motivated by altruistic reasons: the odd case to help out friends or family perhaps, but this is by no means the norm.

- Stop thinking of money as something which has to be put to work for us, as banks continually tell us in their advertising campaigns as if we should feel guilty if this is not a perpetual concern for each and every one of us, but rather treat it as what enables us to live. As noted earlier, Islamic culture has a very different attitude to profit and regards it with considerable suspicion, leading to a system of banking that avoids charging interest on loans. In many ways this appears to be a more mature attitude to adopt, and Islamic banking thinks of itself as being more interested in 'ethical investing, or ethical lending' than the heedless pursuit of profit for its own sake.[31] Other than saving a certain amount, and needing to be protected to some extent against inflation diminishing our savings' value over time, most of us have no need to keep chasing after extra profit through the restless manipulation of whatever financial assets we may have accumulated. If it were to be objected that there are those in our society who do have a need for more profit to guarantee their basic survival, or to lift them out of dire poverty, then the answer would be that they are never going to be in this game anyway: better to seek such results through properly organised social welfare programmes than through the anarchy of the market.

- If you are still a shareholder, however, but perhaps beginning to feel sympathetic towards the anti-profit cause, then use your position to call your company to account if they are being ethically irresponsible. Annual general meetings can provide a platform for this sort of criticism to be voiced, and shareholders can start campaigns amongst other shareholders to make the argument more weighty and more difficult for corporations to sideline with vague promises of reform. Milton Friedman notwithstanding, there is a concept in the business world entitled 'corporate social responsibility' (CSR) that most large corporations claim to be supporters of and that is supposed to go farther than the mere generation of profit, although in far too many cases 'claim' is the operative word and companies are paying it little more than lip service. Breaches of ethics occur rather too frequently for comfort in the business world, with the practice of outsourcing alone generating a host of these, much to the discredit of the Western corporations involved.

A recent case involving Apple indicates just how problematical outsourcing can be on an ethical plane. Foxconn, the company that produces Apple iPads in Shenzhen and Chengdu, China, has been the subject of a scandal over its working practices, which as a report on the company in the Western press put it, reveal 'a Dickensian world of work that would be considered shocking in the West'.[32] In order to keep up with the huge worldwide demand for iPads, assembly-line employees can find themselves working twelve-hour days, with only one day off every thirteen days. Basic daily wages can be as low as £5.20 before overtime. So bad are the conditions that seven workers committed suicide in 2010, and although this did create an outcry around the world, the only substantial reaction of the company has been to install anti-suicide netting around the workers' dormitories and to insist that workers sign a contract to the effect that they promise not to commit suicide while in the company's employ. The contract is less concerned with the individual employee's welfare and more to do with avoiding lawsuits from bereaved families. If globalisation really is a force for good then Western corporations ought to refuse to be party to such practices being carried out in their name, and monitor their suppliers closely to ensure that they are complying. Apple has to be held responsible, therefore, and its record overall with its supplier network is not at all good, as the report on Foxconn goes on to detail:

> The latest figures show Foxconn's Chinese factories are not alone in working staff beyond the legal limits, with fewer than one in three supplier factories obeying the rules on working hours. The audits also show that 30% broke rules on wages and benefits, while 24% were in breach of strict rules on involuntary labour.[33]

Yet the saddest aspect of this case is that Apple is by no means unique. Outsourcing is driven by the desire to maximise profit, not to improve the lifestyle of the developing world's workforce, and the profits that accrue are not negligible: in the first quarter of 2011 alone Apple showed a profit of $6 billion. The notion of 'fair trade' does not seem to have caught on in the computer industry.

- If you are an employee of a company that is guilty of ethical breaches then think about resorting to whistleblowing to make these public, difficult though this undoubtedly can make your life.[34] Whistleblowing will never make you popular with managements, who are most likely to close ranks against you and treat you as the enemy – as might even your co-workers, whose jobs may well be threatened by any subsequent action taken against the company by the authorities. There is no denying that it constitutes a career-threatening move, but the loyalty of the anti-profiteer has to lie elsewhere – with the public, and his or her conscience, instead of with the employer.

- Consider slowing down your life so that you can appreciate the value of human relationships more than the pursuit of profit. This is yet another practical way of curing our addiction to profit. There is a series of movements which have adopted this agenda in recent years: 'Slow Food' and 'Slow City' being among the most prominent. The goal is always the same: to steer us away from the notion that 'time is money', and the attendant belief that unless we are engaged in some profit-generating exercise or other then we are wasting a precious resource and falling behind our peers in the neoliberal rat race. Slow Food campaigners argue that we should take pleasure in the activity of eating itself, seeing it as a social occasion wherever possible, rather than to regard it as merely a necessary refuelling break in a driven lifestyle that must be resumed as quickly as possible to keep up the momentum. The latter is the image that invariably comes to mind with the American fast food model, which seems intent on conquering the globe these days – the well-documented phenomenon of 'McDonaldisation'. Slow City similarly wants us all just to calm down, to cut back on our addiction to a hectic lifestyle that can turn cities into such exhausting, enervating places in which to live.

- Opting out of the rat race is something that anti-profiteers could give serious consideration to as well, even if only for short periods. We could all use regular sabbaticals from our work life to travel more extensively, broaden our experience, develop our talents, etc., and we should strive to achieve them where we can. A Slow Career movement sounds like a good idea, connecting us to a network of people who have already made such a decision and can pass on useful advice as to how to cope with the issues that are likely to arise. Most of us treat work as the really important part of our existence, and workaholism is a recognised feature of Western culture, with the UK particularly noted for this. Managements generally approve of workaholism, regarding it as a mark of ambition on the part of the individual, and even subtly encourage it. The tendency is to think that our careers will flounder otherwise, that we will fall behind and others will overtake us in the pursuit of promotion and thus personal financial gain.

- Even more extreme actions that could be taken on our part, so let's at least briefly consider what some of these might be – with the proviso that their practicality might be doubtful. We might avoid the whole 'career' enterprise in the first place, whereby we buy into the corporate ideology and structure our lives on trying to get ahead within the commercial world; such competition would be ruled out. Maybe we should keep changing jobs rather than becoming stuck in any particular career path? Maybe we should do the minimum we can get away with at work, since doing more only increases company profits? What we should be doing at all times is thinking of ways to make the pursuit of profit difficult for those in financial power, putting as many obstacles in their way as we could as a point of ideological principle. Opting out of the market system wherever possible would cut down profits if enough of us were to do so. Perhaps the ultimate logic of the localism argument that so many critics of contemporary capitalism espouse would be to revert to being hunter-gatherers, and indeed that is not so far away from what so many of the more radical green activists are campaigning for in their attempt to turn the clock back on the advanced capitalist lifestyle. It is possible to live more off the land than we currently do, and those who drop out of the rat race tend to pride themselves on doing so, on being as self-sufficient as possible and finding 'food for free'.

At some point we would have to address the issue of civil disobedience when countering the relentless pressure exerted on social relations by the profit empire. As we can see from the anti-privatisation riots in Bolivia, such a response can be justified but comes at a price the public really should not have to bear. Both the anti-capitalism and anti-cuts movements have had to face up to the fact that there are lines that cannot be crossed in terms of protest, and at least in the West there are always other channels that can be used to voice such protests. In the developing world, sadly enough, violent protest is often the only way of making the ruling powers pay any attention to your plight. When events like this happen, then the privatisers, who are all too often Western-generated multinationals, surely have a duty to back down and leave the stage. What was particularly disgraceful in the Bolivian example was the lawsuit subsequently brought against the government by the Bechtel Corporation as if the loss of life in complaining about their pricing policies could simply be ignored. Profit was clearly being put ahead of human life here in a glaring example of the narrowness of vision of the corporate outlook. For the IMF and World Bank to go on demanding the implementation of privatisation policies after such events indicates a similar lack of humanity.

Whether one agrees or disagrees with the principle of civil disobedience, it is always likely to occur in cases of desperation such as applied in Bolivia, bringing the possibility of violence in its wake. It has to be considered a symptom of what is wrong in terms of social relations rather than a cure, whatever political radicals may think. Ideological fault lines are exposed at such times, and any victory that results will ring hollow if it is achieved at the cost of violence and loss of life. In cases like this, however, the real culprit is neoliberalism, which is creating the conditions for such a sense of desperation to arise. Civil disobedience will always be the last resort of the disaffected, but if neoliberalism acts in a cavalier enough fashion, as it is well capable of doing when untapped sources of profit come into view, then it runs the risk of triggering just such a response.

Conclusion: Feeding an Addiction

If James Murdoch was right about our natural gravitation towards profit then we would expect it to be even more pronounced if performance-related pay schemes were introduced into our workplace.

That is the assumption behind the bonus system which the banks, amongst many others in the corporate world, appear to regard as an indispensable part of the higher executive contract these days. Such personnel are routinely awarded enormous annual bonuses on top of already well above the average basic wages, and argue that they would not feel the same sense of urgency to push themselves to increase their employer's profit margins in the 'alpha' category without incentives like this being on offer. In such circles it is, as one commentator on the system has put it, 'almost unquestioned dogma that people are motivated by rewards, so they don't feel the need to test this'.[35] Yet recent studies tend to cast doubt on this dogma and to suggest that, far from improving performance, such schemes might have no effect at all, or even come to affect individual performance adversely. People do not always conceive of work as primarily a means to increase their own financial gain, and are in fact often motivated by factors other than mere financial reward. Anti-profiteers might consider starting campaigns against performance-related pay at their places of work because of the false message it communicates about us. Perhaps they may even come up with suggestions for more socially useful ways of using the money budgeted for these schemes. If work is not always engaged in for reasons of profit, what other 'profitless' activities can we identify that might lead us to question the notion that the term *homo economicus* really does capture our essential character?

3
'What Shall It Profit a Man?': Profitless Activities

The charity business and the voluntary sector invite examination, since it seems likely that it is compassion rather than desire for worldly gain that draws people into participation in these. Religious belief is another obvious area to invite scrutiny, as well as the distorting effect that the profit motive can have on organised religion. This is particularly the case in America with the phenomenon of televangelism, which has turned into a really big business there, a sub-branch of show business in effect. I'll also be considering what the impact might be of reorganising our emotional lives on the profit principle, and whether we could live with the consequences – and if not, why not? The untenability, and even absurdity, of doing so will soon become apparent, but the question then arises as to why we have allowed the profit motive to come to exercise such a hold over our culture when it patently does not cover all our psychological or emotional needs. Why privilege one of our drives so much over the others, especially when it has little application to the greater part of our existence? Who really benefits from this, and do we have to follow their instructions?

Charities and the Voluntary Sector

Charities are a well-established part of Western culture, and they depend very heavily on public goodwill, both for donations and for voluntary work in running them. Some do have full-time paid staff, as in the case of the larger ones like Oxfam; but without voluntary input most would find it difficult to exist, or at the very least find it much harder to generate enough income to pass on anything very substantial to their particular cause. Oxfam shops are staffed by volunteers who contribute so many hours of their time on a regular basis, and because of this it is able to operate a nationwide network of outlets ensuring a high level of public recognition that creates both a solid donor and customer base.

Oxfam is a big business, with a turnover on donated goods alone of £67.1 million annually (2009–10), so it is clearly held in high regard by the general public which has been passing on used clothes and household items to it for seventy years now.[1] It is only one of a host of similar charities using that operating model, accepting discarded items for sale to raise money for their particular concern, whatever that may be – children, heart disease, mental illness, etc. Whatever profit they make is achieved through the goodwill of the public, who identify in one way or another with the cause in question and are happy to see any profits that they help to generate, either as donor or buyer of goods, put to such good social use. When individuals are seen to make profit from such activities, as in cases brought to light of charity-shop clothing being sold by private entrepreneurs in various African markets, then there can be public unease about this. Even though the charities involved have made money from selling off the merchandise that they will go on to use for their respective good causes, the feeling persists that it is wrong for this to lead to private profit: that would never be the intention of the donors, and when such stories hit the press they create bad publicity for the charities which can affect their business for a while.

Neither do we restrict ourselves just to giving away unwanted items and occasionally shopping in Oxfam, etc., stores. We also commit ourselves voluntarily to monthly or annual donations by way of direct debit to organisations like the Red Cross; again, in the belief that what they do is socially important and deserving of our private support. In that sense the 'Big Society' that the UK coalition government is promoting already exists, and no one is denying that it is a good thing which provides an outlet for our feelings of social responsibility, inviting us to see beyond our own narrow self-interest and think in terms of the community and those less fortunate than ourselves. All that is at issue over the notion of the Big Society at present is whether the voluntary sector should be an addition to, or an alternative to, public welfare underwritten by tax money. It is when it is perceived as the latter, essentially as a way of cutting public spending for ideological reasons, the latest neoliberal wheeze, that the problems arise, as I shall go on to discuss in later chapters.

Other voluntary organisations can be more politically minded, as in the case of Amnesty International, which fights for the cause of those imprisoned, or tortured, by tyrannical regimes around the globe. Many of us see this as a crucial supplement to formal politics, which has a much wider brief to take care of and cannot devote much time or resource to following up such individual cases in detail. The scale of the problem is such that unless there is a scheme dedicated to monitoring what happens on this front then most of the abuses will simply go unnoticed and unreported, so appealing for public financial support makes sense: such activities cannot really be catered for properly by the public sector. While governments can make general statements about the need to respect human rights, there is a limit as to what they can do about individual instances of breaches of these in other countries: certain diplomatic niceties have to be observed otherwise relations can break down altogether. A strong case can be made, therefore, for circumventing the public sector on this occasion, and adopting what we could call a Big Society approach, involving us at the level of individual conscience, in order to supplement the official line on human rights.

I mentioned above about public unease at discovering that discarded clothes, etc., can end up for sale in the developing world, thus introducing the profit motive into the enterprise and undermining the charitable ethos to some extent. But something even more problematical is occurring at present in the UK as a direct result of neoliberal policy. The current round of spending cuts to reduce the financial industry-created national budget deficit is forcing local councils to look for new ways to raise cash on their assets. Some have turned to charging ground rent for recycling banks, for clothing as a case in point, on council-owned land such as rubbish tips. Previously, these were collected by charities like the British Heart Association and Scope (collecting for cerebral palsy), but now councils are expecting to be paid for them which has meant that for-profit organisations such as Nathans Wastesavers and Cookstown Textile Recycling have stepped into the breach. Scope's director has complained bitterly about this new policy:

> We understand that all councils have to make tough spending decisions, but asking charities to start paying for using textile banks is a worrying move. Charities are easy targets, but the consequences are serious. If many more councils follow suit, this could seriously undermine a vital and popular source of fundraising for charities.[2]

Scope alone stands to lose around £150,000 in annual sales from its shops in the areas run by the two councils trialling the scheme, Hertfordshire and Northumberland, the recycling banks of which will now generate profit for the councils and private companies involved. This is exactly how things should be as far as neoliberalism is concerned, councils should be as profit-conscious as possible and private enterprise must be brought into the process wherever that is possible. So even our charitable impulses are to be regarded as potential profit centres, although the logical conclusion to this would be that we should start charging for donating our unwanted items to for-profit private companies; at which point we are no longer talking about charity of course, but commercial bargaining for the purpose of maximising our assets. Everything is fair game as far as neoliberalism goes, and the more profit-conscious we become the better. Profit's empire seems relentlessly to expand.

Religion and the Profit Motive

Televangelism is where religion meets the profit motive in a big way, with the earnings to be made from success in this area being very considerable: far more than the standard that a career clergyman employed by the average established church can ever hope to achieve. Religion in America is in general a very prosperous business, which has combined the American commercial creed with the nation's perceived spiritual needs to striking effect. From modest beginnings back in the 1950s and 60s televangelism now has a well-established place in American life, with its leading figures like show-business stars with their own loyal following, and it is very profitable, coining in substantial advertising revenues on top of donations. It has never caught on to the same extent in Europe, however, despite periodic attempts to break into the market. Although the globally highly successful GOD-TV, claiming half a billion viewers internationally, started in the UK, it eventually moved its headquarters to Jerusalem, and is far more popular in the USA than it is in the UK. In terms of the scale and proliferation of channels, televangelism is a predominantly American phenomenon, and that is certainly where the big profits are to be made in the medium.

Money is never far from the scene in the televangelism world, with viewers being constantly exhorted to contribute to the church's funds or social programmes on a regular basis, even if this sometimes strays into the realms of the absurd, as it did with the preacher Oral Roberts in 1987. One of the biggest names on the circuit, having been broadcasting since the 1940s, Roberts claimed that God would 'call him home' if he did not raise $8 million dollars by a specified date, and duly reported the figure reached each day towards that total to his fascinated viewers as the clock ticked down. When it did not look like the total would be reached in time, Roberts said God had granted him an extension, and while one might have thought this would have dented his credibility, and that of televangelism in general, it didn't seem to and he eventually managed to raise $9.1 million. In fact the televangelism market has proved itself to be more or less impervious to the scandals its stars have been caught up in over the years; scandals which have taken in such anti-moral majority behaviour as adultery, homosexuality, and consorting with prostitutes. One would have thought that exploiting religious beliefs to make a profit would also come into that latter category of being anti-Christian, but there seems to be a blind spot about that in America.

The link between money and belief in the American religious world has been made very explicit by the doctrine of 'Prosperity Theology'. This holds that God rewards his believers with financial success, and indeed there is a history of this belief in the Protestant tradition in the Anglo-Saxon world. Nonconformists in late seventeenth-century and eighteenth-century England often thought similarly; excluded from the universities and most of the professions by their beliefs, many entered into business and trade and interpreted economic success there as a sign of God's approval. The highly prosperous stars of televangelism would seem to provide visible proof of the truth of this link in a contemporary America which has more than something of a fixation with financial success. From Oral Roberts onwards, they have had a tendency to flaunt their wealth in a luxurious lifestyle which their audience appears to find quite acceptable, and perhaps even expects to see. One of the leading exponents of this doctrine is Bishop T. D. Jakes, whose take on prosperity theology has at least some claim to credibility in that he envisages it as a way of trying to close the economic gap that exists between white Americans and African Americans. There is no denying that it has made him personally successful, since as well as being pastor of a megachurch, a popular televangelist and best-selling author, he has a portfolio of business interests including a record label. Perhaps the only sure-fire way to be rewarded by God is to become a televangelism star.

While it is easy to satirise such a phenomenon as televangelism, as many American social commentators and comedians frequently do, there is no doubt that it is a potent combination that appeals to many millions of the American population, as well as increasingly to a worldwide audience.[3] The fundamentalist temperament has no difficulty encompassing both profit and religion.

Televangelism is an essentially Protestant field, but that does not mean that other forms of Christianity are untouched by the profit motive. The Roman Catholic Church, as a case in point, is one of the world's richest institutions, holding assets worth billions of dollars. Profit is not its main reason for existence of course, but it does very well nevertheless out of the income that it generates and is not averse to operating in the financial world, to the extent of running its own bank. Religion here is by no means a profitless phenomenon, even if the concern is to use profit in a generally humanitarian way rather than for any individual's personal gain. Having said that, the Vatican Bank, which is famed for its secrecy, has been the subject of considerable controversy over the years, including charges of money laundering on various occasions. The Vatican state is a member of neither the EU nor the IMF so it is free of the auditing controls associated with those institutions. This is a situation which makes the Vatican Bank – or to give it its altogether grander-sounding official name, the Institute for Works of Religion – an attractive proposition for investors of dubious repute, showing the murky waters that religion can find itself getting into when it openly embraces the commercial world.

Most churches have considerable financial assets, even if only in property, and most invest their money in profit-making projects of one kind or another in order to fund the many activities they undertake in the community. All of them have a business dimension, in other words, and regard that as a perfectly normal part of their affairs. The Anglican Church, which is generally perceived to have been in a state of decline for some time now in the UK, is nevertheless still financially buoyant. In the accounts for 2008, for example, the Church Commissioners were reported to be managing assets of £4.4 billion with a wide portfolio of investments. Despite these investments having been hit by the fall in share values in the aftermath of the credit crisis, many being in the volatile property market, they were providing 15 per cent of the organisation's annual running costs, so profit has an important role to play in the Church's everyday existence.[4]

Emotion and Profit

If we were to start running our emotional lives with an eye to profit then we would be compelled to look at the world and our fellow human beings very differently than we do now. There may of course be some cold-hearted individuals out there who already organise themselves in that fashion, putting financial gain before emotional satisfaction: what would we need to do to swell their ranks and extend profit's empire even further? The comments that follow are intended to be taken ironically, but in the fashion of Deleuze and Guattari they may make us think a bit more deeply about the implications of the ideology we are currently living by.

The West tends to be critical of the concept of arranged marriage, which is still common in many Asian societies, but surely that would be the way forward if we were to shift wholeheartedly to a profit orientation, checking beforehand to ensure that our financial position was significantly improved by the prospective match. This is the way that many dynastic marriages were set up in the West's past, until quite recent times as a matter of fact, and if profit were to be the major criterion of suitability then it would be a method well worth resurrecting as a general practice. If our bodies are indeed property to be sold on the open market in order to make profit for ourselves, as we are constantly being told we should consider them to be under a capitalist regime, then there is no logical reason why this principle should not be adhered to in all areas of our lives.[5] It is even possible to construct an argument in defence of prostitution using this principle, as Janet Radcliffe Richards provocatively suggested in her book *The Sceptical Feminist*.[6]

With birth control widely available we are no longer at the mercy of our biology as our forebears were until only a few generations ago, but many couples still choose to have children. Children have in the past been considered sources of profit in a way, with their labour power being an important factor in a peasant family's survival, for example: at subsistence level it makes sense to have more help in this fashion, and also to have a resource to fall back on in one's old age as a parent. In the modern West, however, this no longer applies, and in real terms children are a drain on any parent's budget. Aside from food and clothing, which constitutes an increasing burden as children grow up, childcare is very expensive if the parents both wish to go on working or to have a social life outside the home. Given the progressive retreat of the state from being the major funding source of higher education, that is also a drain that is likely to continue much further into parents' lives than hitherto: the phenomenon of stay-at-home children in their twenties, and even thirties, has been remarked on frequently by social commentators in recent years. Looked at coldly and unemotionally, children make no financial sense, and would have to be seen as a personal indulgence: whatever reasons there may be for having them, profit cannot be one of them.

Friendship should be seen as another area where we need to revise our principles and procedures. Friends surely should be above all financially useful, either helping in one's career or in one's general financial dealings, otherwise they represent wasted personal effort on our part. We would have to accept that others will want to view us in this light too, as a resource, but at the very least we should ensure that any such relationship that we do decide to enter into is mutually beneficial: profit must always be in the forefront of our minds or else we shall start to fall behind our competitive peers, and that will not be good for our career prospects.

We need to be very careful, too, about our choice of career if we are going to maximise our lifetime earnings. Anything to do with public service should be strongly resisted: this is rarely going to be very well paid, and certainly not for the rank and file.[7] Such employment calls for the wrong kind of mindset anyway, one oriented towards service to others rather than personal profit. Since we are now being required to fund most of our own higher education we should make sure that we choose something that is directly vocational to study; in which case arts and humanities subjects should be ruled out, as most social science ones should be too. Even if some arts subjects might appear vocational in the creative line, they are rarely a good bet for secure, regular earnings; not unless you reach the superstar level. There is no point studying anything which does not offer you a definite career structure with substantial rewards attached from the beginning: once educated, you need to start earning well very quickly if you are to repay your fees debt in any reasonable length of time. One suspects that this is precisely the kind of attitude that the government wants to encourage in us, that this would represent the neoliberal ideal for higher education: a firmly business-oriented graduate class concerned to maximise their earning potential, and thus, according to the neoliberal creed, increase the national wealth.

Irony aside, it may well be, as I suggested earlier, that there are individuals out there who conduct their lives according to principles such as the ones just discussed, and who are guided above all in their relations with others by thought of personal financial profit. But would the rest of us want to know such people, be friendly with them, fall in love with them? More likely, we would just consider them to be completely mercenary and find them difficult to relate to on anything other than a strictly business basis, which surely has to represent some sort of argument against the Murdoch line.

Conclusion

There is no doubt that we could if we put our minds to it transform a whole raft of profitless activities in our lives into profit-centred ones, and increase our personal wealth if we did so systematically enough. The only problem is that to obey the dictates of finance in this fashion would go against the grain of how most of us are emotionally constructed, preferring in several areas of our lives to be led by feelings of love, friendship, and compassion rather than by financial factors; in other words by our social instincts rather than our supposed profit ones. Indeed, most of us would say that our humanity is revealed by the expression of such feelings and that we would be lesser beings were we to eradicate them from our natures, or even relegate them to secondary considerations beneath our financial desires. But if even charity can be colonised by the forces of profit then we may have something of a struggle on our hands to hold on to our better instincts. As I shall go on to discuss next, there have been instances of societies in which profit did not loom as large in everyday life as it does now, even societies minus the profit motive altogether, but the current socio-economic regime seems determined to erase that from the collective memory.

4
Life Before Profit, Life Minus Profit

Societies based on the profit motive are a very recent phenomenon in human history. It can be salutary to reflect on that fact and also to ask ourselves whether we have anything to learn from these earlier, pre-capitalist, societies, despite our undeniably more advanced, technologically anyway, state. What, for example, was the major ideological focus of classical culture, or pre-modern Christian and Islamic societies? It was not profit as we understand it nowadays, even if wealth and trading did play their part and individuals and families clearly did benefit from these activities. The religious aspect, so important in the latter two cases, may not have relevance to all of us any more, nor the tendency of all three towards fairly rigid social hierarchies where everyone was expected to keep their place; but are there perhaps positive aspects of pre-capitalist societies that we could adapt to our purposes now in a campaign to counter the ideological tyranny exercised over our lives by profit? If there are, then might these help us to rethink our current criteria for assessing value, and so shift away from our overwhelmingly economic bias? To make us recognise that we could organise our life around different criteria if we so chose? As one commentator has so pointedly put it as regards current campaigns to encourage universities to cash in on their research in order to make up for cuts in government funding: 'how can money be used to assess a valuable new insight into Shakespeare as he wrote his plays, or the social changes

43

that led to the first flowerings of democracy in Ancient Greece?'[1] It is a question well worth mulling over. But the main point being made is one that transcends education, and it is that there are kinds of value other than the economic, and that perhaps these are more important than the economic in terms of our development as individuals and as a culture.

This should not be construed as an argument for a return to the pre-modern, as this would hardly be practical or even practicable. Rather it is a call for recognition that economic self-interest is not the only thing holding society together, no matter what neo-liberal apologists may say, and that we ought to work harder to create institutions and systems within our culture that enable us to develop and share all the non-economic needs that we plainly have: that is, as we shall go on to see in the next chapter, the conclusion reached by the RSA Social Brain project amongst others. And it is the institutions already filling such a function in our society that are most under threat from the current turn against public spending in the West. A plea for greater responsibility and more of a sense of public conscience in the uses to which wealth creation is put does not constitute nostalgia for the pre-modern lifestyle, but rather a change of direction to the current ideological paradigm that is well within our power to make.

The tendency of late in the West is to assume that almost all our needs must be subordinated to the economic, that once this dimension is sorted out then everything else will more or less fall into place. Most politicians are obsessed with the economy as their primary responsibility, regarding it as central to their electoral success; that is even the case at present when political parties are having to admit that cutting the national deficit, and hence the living standards of the majority of the population, is a necessary step to take post-election. The line generally taken is that once this has been achieved, *then* we can move back to economic stability and resumed growth, which must always be our paramount concern as a society. Hence the drive to ensure that public institutions are opened up to the profit motive, the argument being that this will be to our greater benefit; they will become more efficient, more entrepreneurial in spirit, thus less costly. Yet we know that societies can be run differently, as history amply demonstrates. Even if we accept that the profit motive is not likely to disappear altogether, we can alter how profit itself is used and shared around, and in a general sense, perceived. Profit is not our god, and we have no need to treat it as such: however, it is our addiction, and we do need to treat it as such, whether we are of a reformist or a radical persuasion.

At the moment, however, most politicians are in still in thrall to the Friedmanite 'trickle-down' conception of wealth creation, and while this is true up to a point, the extent of the 'trickle' ought to be the subject of far more vigorous public debate to ensure that lack of wealth does not disqualify one from access to critically important areas such as healthcare or higher education.[2] Otherwise we end up with ever growing disparities between those who construct their lives around wealth creation and those who do not or cannot, with the former setting the terms of reference for how society in general operates, which these days has developed into a hyper-possessive individualism consistently privileging the private good over the public. It is even possible to argue that what neoliberalism results in is a 'trickle up' effect, which accentuates disparity. The more of that disparity we have then the more insistently that social tension and class envy arises, and that is not a healthy state of affairs for a democracy to find itself in. The notion that a profit-led society is our destiny as a species urgently needs to be countered, therefore, as does the idea that profit belongs to the individual rather than to our culture in general. Again, it is a case of restating what we have gained from the introduction of socialist principles into Western society, of reminding us how these have helped to reduce social injustice, to everyone's benefit, and what we run the risk of losing should we fail to prevent neoliberalism from dismantling these altogether on the most spurious of ideological grounds.

It will be pertinent, too, to explore what went wrong in those systems in modern times that did make a concerted effort to de-individualise profit, and speculate on whether such failures could have been avoided, whether a profitless society could actually be made to work and successfully meet the whole range of human social needs: life minus profit. Communism presents an interesting test case in this respect.

The World Pre-Profit

It is important to point out that by 'pre-profit' I do not mean to indicate that pre-modern societies had no concept of this at all, since people did trade and invest in various kinds of enterprise that did make money. I am referring instead to pre-'Profit', the world of profit addiction that we now inhabit. One has to be careful not to idealise older societies, however, to picture them purely on the basis of their best qualities while conveniently ignoring the often numerous negative ones. Classical Greek culture is a relevant example of how this can happen. We can praise Athens for its development of democratic principles and for fostering a vibrant intellectual life that established the Western philosophical tradition, while forgetting that democracy was not extended to the majority of the population of the city state. Women, predictably enough, were excluded altogether. Then there is the uncomfortable fact that much of Athens' wealth came from the labour of a slave community, estimated to have been as large as 20,000, working in its silver mines; this in a city with around 60,000 citizens. We also have to remember that democracy was not a permanent feature of the state's history, and that in its supposed 'golden age' Athens swung back and forth between that political system and various autocratic and tyrannical regimes. So we have to accept that when we speak of official attitudes or an ideological paradigm we are only referring to the actions of an elite. Let's consider what ideals motivated that dominant group and what it was that they most valued in terms of public life, as well as how these compare with the ones that generally apply in our own time.

What strikes us immediately when looking at that Athenian elite is how highly they seemed to prize knowledge for its own sake, and how concerned their philosophers were with the concept of virtue, both in its public and private guises: Socrates, Plato, and Aristotle, to take the outstanding examples. There was an emphasis on developing a moral character and living morally because this was the right thing to do, rather than because one had some kind of hidden agenda, such as a desire to make oneself look good in the public eye in order to gain some personal benefit. These are still ideals we would claim for own culture, but although hardly anyone is going to argue against knowledge or virtue in any abstract sense, increasingly the tendency is to value the former for its profit-generating potential and to regard the pursuit of profit as a public virtue in itself – its 'guarantor' if we take the Murdoch line of argument. The 'good life' seen from that last perspective is the one that is guided by profit, and where the role of the social systems is to help expedite this with as little fuss as possible: in effect, to stay out of the way of entrepreneurial activity and to let it develop as those engaged in it see fit. Whether acting in this way constitutes enough of a virtue to hold society together and provide everyone within it with a route to the 'good life' has to remain highly problematical. That is not how the leading lights of classical Greece pictured social existence, and we do seem to have lost something crucial in our moral sense along the way since then if it is the desire for profit that is the imperative dictating our actions and underpinning our social being instead.

Neither would I wish to idealise pre-modern life in its medieval form. But again we are struck by the ideals it thought itself to be living by, with religious and spiritual matters being strongly emphasised; these being, as far as we are concerned nowadays, metaphysical concerns rather than the insistently material ones that have since come to dominate social existence in the West. It is possible to envisage an existence where profit is not the primary factor in dictating people's public behaviour, including the institutions they proceed to develop, or their private desires.

Islamic societies are amongst the best examples of theocratic regimes in the modern/postmodern world, and they certainly are motivated by metaphysical concerns, especially when they espouse Shari'ah law, which imposes a religious dimension on all human conduct. The West has long since rejected theocracy, and I am by no means recommending it here; but it is yet another example of a lifestyle based on factors other than the economic that appears to satisfy a significant percentage of the globe's population, even though many of them are living in some of the world's poorest countries. Not all of humanity sees profit as its destiny; lifestyles can be constructed on the basis of other reasons, although there is more than a certain irony in the fact that those Islamic countries with large oil reserves do make enormous profits out of selling this natural resource to the West, and as a result contain some of the world's richest people. Even if the oil runs out they may be able to continue raking profits in on the basis of solar power, a topic I'll be dealing with in Chapter 7.

Nevertheless, Islam as a system still finds profit problematical, and Islamic banks are forbidden to charge interest, leading to some complex regulations about how loans are administered that have to accord with the terms of Shari'ah law:

> Islam argues that there is no justifiable reason why a person should enjoy an increase in wealth from the use of his money by another, unless he is prepared to expose his wealth to the risk of loss also. Islam views true profit as a return for entrepreneurial effort and objects to money being placed on a pedestal above labour, the other factor in production. As long as the owner of money is willing to become a shareholder in the enterprise and expose his money to the risk of loss, he is entitled to receive a just proportion of the profits and not merely a merely nominal share based on the prevailing interest rate.[3]

Islamic banking is thus committed to a partnership system in which profit has to be morally justified, describing itself as being concerned to encourage cooperation amongst principals in order 'to eliminate exploitation and to establish a just society'.[4] This would seem to call for a practice which is a far cry from the wilder goings-on of the money markets in the West, particularly in the latter days of the pre-credit crisis boom period. In fact, that crisis sparked an upturn of interest in the world financial system about Islamic banking, given that it seemed far less sensitive to market turmoil than Western banks clearly were.

Although Islamic banking is widely practised in the Islamic world, it still constitutes only a small share of the global banking industry. How true it always is to Qur'anic principles in all its busi-ness dealings is a matter of conjecture – it can hardly avoid contact with the Western banking system altogether in an era of globalisa-tion after all, and that invites at least a degree of pragmatism to be shown, quite possibly leading to some slippage from doctrinal purity. Yet Islamic banking remains interesting in having to justify those dealings by factors other than economic necessity, which might be seen as some kind of safeguard against the anarchy that we otherwise experience in the West. The pressure to keep your money 'working' for you seems less evident in the Islamic system, and as I suggested earlier, this could be seen to constitute a more mature attitude towards our assets.

There is an element of social responsibility implicit in Islamic banking, therefore, that is sadly missing in its Western counterpart, and we could well learn a lesson from it. Ensuring that responsibil-ity is upheld by the banks is the duty of appointed boards made up of Shari'ah scholars. The idea of Western banking practices being monitored by theologians is a piquant one, but it could reason-ably be expected that boards of directors paid more attention to the ethical aspects of investing than purely to ensuring that share-holders' dividends were increased; that they acted as some kind of conscience to their business in the manner that Sharia'h scholars do. Anything that holds out the promise of making credit crises less likely to happen has to be worth investigating, and Islamic bank-ing's goal of offering 'a balance between extreme capitalism and communism' seems to strike the right kind of note in the current cultural climate.[5]

The Green Movement: The End of the Modern and the End of Profit?

The Green movement is such a diffuse phenomenon that it is very difficult to generalise on it; but if most Green activists are seeking reform of our political system to keep environmental pollution and despoliation in check, then at least some of the movement's more extreme elements are also calling for an end to the progress-driven, thus also profit-driven, culture that currently is the norm. The idea of returning to a simpler lifestyle, more localised in set-up and most likely agrarian in character, can sound quite seductive in a culture in which constant, unremitting change has become the standard. Behind it lies the belief that industrialisation was the point at which things started to go horribly wrong in our relationship to our planet. Societies throughout history have had a tendency to idealise the past – think of the reverence for classical culture in the Renaissance period, for example, when it was held to be the repository of almost all human wisdom and the measure against which everything in the present was to be judged. If anything, this tendency has become more marked in modern times when the speed of technological and social change can come to seem very bewildering to us as individuals. Modernity and industrialisation may have improved our lifestyles out of all recognition, but they have also had a dislocating effect on our culture to the extent that looking back with nostalgia, often just for a generation or two, has become a common occurrence. In the early to mid-nineteenth century, when a phase of massive expansion of industrialisation throughout Western European life made it an even more disorienting time than our own in terms of the cultural shift that was taking place, there was a cult of medievalism in countries like Britain. Influential thinkers such as Thomas Carlyle presented a picture of medieval life as possessing an intrinsically organic quality that industrialisation and the march of technological progress had all but eliminated, leaving us the poorer as a community. For Carlyle the desire for profit, at the expense of human dignity, lay at the root of the problem. He claimed that medieval life, symbolised for him by institutions such as the monastery, was motivated by altogether nobler ideals than the new industrial age and lacked its obsession with financial gain and ever-increasing levels of production.[6] Monasteries, Carlyle argued, provided a level of support for both the individual's spiritual and material needs which no mass-production factory ever could, the latter regarding its employees merely as 'hands' in a mechanical process and thus interchangeable with each other, as if they had no individual identity of their own.[7] Workers were not alienated from their labour in the medieval context in the way that Marx in particular would go on to rail against as one of the greatest evils of the modern day.

It was an impossibly over-idealised image that was being constructed, taking little account of the well-documented hardships of medieval life. What it does tell us, however, is that change was not viewed as an unproblematically beneficial phenomenon by everyone at the time, and that despite the huge technological improvements coming on stream there was a definite yearning for a less driven kind of lifestyle beginning to develop, a reaction to the shock of the new. It was a yearning that went on to express itself in the introduction of various elements of medievalism into Victorian daily life, with clothing, art and architecture, as cases in point, reflecting a growing popular nostalgia for an assumed simpler and happier age. Edifices like the Gothic-revival Houses of Parliament provide eloquent testimony as to just how deeply embedded such ideas became.

Although not as historically specific in their nostalgia, the more radical Greens represent an extension of such an outlook, turning their back on technological progress and the modern world because of its adverse effect on the environment. The argument is that it will only be with a much smaller population and progressively less reliance on technology that we shall cut down these adverse effects, and thus ensure the survival of the human race. Otherwise, climate change will spiral completely out of our control and we shall find that we have created a global environmental disaster of apocalyptic proportions where the delicate balance of the planet's ecological systems, 'Gaia' as it has been dubbed, simply collapses.[8] What that change means in practice to radical Greens is a small-community, highly localised lifestyle based largely on agricultural production, in which the primary concern is to preserve the environment rather than ruthlessly to exploit it in the name of continually rising living standards – and, of course, continually rising profits for the corporate sector.

It is yet another highly idealised vision, and one that goes resolutely against the grain of our upbringing and cultural training. Yet there is no denying that it speaks to at least some in the West and that it represents a rejection of the profit ethos, even if it is less likely to appeal in the developing world, where in many cases modernity has barely made an impact on the lives of the general population as yet and is much more coveted in consequence. Short of a natural disaster reducing us to that condition, we are highly unlikely to see such a programme being implemented, but it does indicate that opposition to profit is not just the preserve of communists, and that there may well be a much larger constituency out there in the West waiting to hear an anti-profit message. Maybe there is more uneasiness around in our society about where the drive to profit is leading us than either the business world or the political class is willing to admit. In this sense the anti-capitalist and anti-globalisation movements may be just the tip of the iceberg.

Communism and the End of Profit

Communism tried as hard as it could to remove the factor of profit from our economic lives, with the state deciding how these would be conducted and what our respective allotted roles in the process would be, at least ostensibly for the public good. This was to be the era of the command economy, when central planning took over from competing organisations only interested in their own performance and the dividends they could provide for their shareholders through increased profit margins. Profit was equated with exploitation in Marxist thought, the result of capitalists keeping back for themselves, as owners of the means of production, the surplus value that was created by the wage labour of the working classes. Pierre-Joseph Proudhon had famously argued that '[p]roperty was robbery', insisting on the 'perfect identity' between the two, and even if this was asserted from an anarchist perspective it was a sentiment that could also resonate with Marxists, for whom profit in general was effectively a robbery from each individual worker by the capitalist class.[9] If the state ran the means of production on behalf of the workers, however, then such theft would be eradicated. That, at any rate, was the assumption made by Marxist theoreticians. All surplus value would then be used by the state to improve the workers' lot and everyone in a communist society would gain equally from the improvements subsequently made, rather than wealth being the province of only an elite few, as it plainly was in a capitalist society. The communist system was organised around that principle, which was immediately put into practice whenever communists took over a previously market-based state, as in Russia in 1917 and then in its post-Second World War Eastern European satellites and Maoist China.

In reality, living standards in the communist world failed abysmally to keep pace with those in the West, and the command economy failed to deliver on a reliable basis even the most basic goods that an advanced society requires. Food shortages were a standard feature of life under communism right up to the collapse of the Soviet empire, with other everyday items such as clothing also being in perennially short supply. Improvements in living standards in the West, on the other hand, could be presented as the public pay-off for a profit-based system which admittedly benefitted some more than others. Historical circumstances have to be taken into account as regards Russia, of course, and it has to be conceded that for most of the Soviet Union's seventy-odd years of existence it was confronted by a hostile world that was doing its very best to overturn the system, culminating in the decades-long Cold War of the later twentieth century which the Soviet system ultimately could not sustain, such were the disparities in national wealth between there and the West. Such opposition makes it hard to determine whether a non-profit regime like this is intrinsically unworkable, or whether under the right conditions it could be made to function for the public good and thus win enough popular support to develop further. Would it have worked better, for example, if it had not felt the need to guarantee its security by the diversion of so much resource into armaments for defence? After all, the Cold War all but demanded such a policy on the Soviet's part. It seems entirely likely that it would have developed differently, especially given the massive investment that the space race required to keep pace with America, its capitalist mirror image; investment which would undoubtedly have gone a long way towards improving the general living standards of the Soviet population.

For all its deep-seated flaws, the communist system can nevertheless evoke feelings of nostalgia in quite a few people in the countries of the ex-Soviet empire after exposure to the ways of Western capitalism. The imposition of the profit ethic has not always meant an improvement in the quality of life, particularly amongst those at the lower end of the socio-economic scale. Those at that level have often found welfare provision, including pensions, savagely slashed as their governments are required to cut public spending in return for aid from the IMF, which invariably makes such demands on debtor countries. The need to make the national economy favourable to big business tends to override all other considerations, and many suffer in the wake of that policy. Granted, many others also find their lifestyle and prospects improved immeasurably on the economic front, but that merely translates into ever-growing disparities of wealth in such societies, exactly what we are becoming increasingly aware of as one of the most problematical side effects of the neoliberal regime in the West. Predictably enough, it is public sector workers who are most badly hit as the neoliberal doctrine of public provision bad, private provision good is put into full-blown practice. With healthcare and education being particularly affected, communism can come to have an unexpected appeal in retrospect, even to appear more socially conscious. Neoliberalism is never the best advert for the capitalist system.

In its early days, the Soviet state did genuinely seem to generate popular support with its promise of a new kind of society that had broken decisively with the past, and it remains one of the saddest aspects of the Soviet revolution that the goodwill that was plainly there in that period was so recklessly squandered by the communist party. It is always going to be problematical to claim, as the latter-day far left often still does, that Stalinism constitutes a perversion of Marxist doctrine and that it does not have to develop in that particular way with its oppressively authoritarian bias. The impact of particular individuals cannot be discounted, yet the possibility that Marxism leads to totalitarianism has to be considered, and there is evidence to suggest that many aspects of the theory do in fact push it in that direction – if not necessarily to the extent of Stalinism.[10] Whether it can be revised to prevent that happening is another question.

We know from the example of China that Marxist-communism can be adapted to include other ideological doctrines, even if China still insists on a highly centralised system of political control that recalls the Soviet system in the many petty restrictions it places on personal freedoms. The pursuit of profit is allowed, therefore, but it is by no means clear that this alone is going to be enough to placate the population for the lack of those freedoms, and that life minus profit would not work if those freedoms were to be granted. People are capable of working for the public good without thinking of personal profit, as we know from the experience of various religious groupings, kibbutzes, and organisations of like sort; but that commitment has to involve free choice and not coercion by the state. It must also include the right to opt in and out as the individual decides; again, coercion, or force of any kind, merely destroys the altruistic impulse that would lead one to want to be part of something greater than oneself and to devote one's energies selflessly towards the success of such a project. The extent to which that impulse motivates us constitutes the next topic for consideration.

5

Profit in the Genes?

Philosophers, scientists, and sociologists have debated heatedly over the years as to whether human beings are naturally competitive or cooperative, programmed to be social animals or self-interested individuals. Theories come and go, but none of them seems to be provable beyond all reasonable doubt. To a large extent what is emphasised at any one point historically tends to be motivated primarily by ideological concerns. When communism was being developed from Marx and Engels through into the Soviet era, then its theorists looked around for evidence of our social-cooperative nature and took anything that they could find in this line to be defining of human nature. In more recent times, Richard Dawkins' *The Selfish Gene* has sought out reasons to support altruism as a basis for social existence, and something very similar is also coming through in the Royal Society for the encouragement of Arts, Manufactures and Commerce (RSA) Social Brain project, which has been running since 2009. Both of these projects will be considered below. In the business world, however, hard-line versions of Darwinism picturing life as a constant struggle still find an audience, and serve to reinforce the neoliberal view of us as essentially competitive-individualist: 'All of us are living under Darwin's design requirements, perpetually forced to come up with new moves to win the next round of marketplace competition.'[1] Thomas Hobbes had reached a similar conclusion in the early days of modern culture, arguing in *Leviathan* that self-interest was our basic drive.[2] In each case, a form of society is devised, or at least strongly recommended as worth developing, to enable us to make the most out of what are assumed to be our natural traits: our social existence being tailored to our programming.

It seems more likely that we have both these drives in our make-up and that either can be emphasised – and the decision to go one way or the other will be heavily influenced by ideological factors. The bias here in this chapter, as it almost invariably is in leftist thought, will be to the social-cooperative side on the grounds that altruistic and cooperative behaviour is more beneficial to society at large than the self-interested individualism implicit in the very notion of *homo economicus*; but the chapter as a whole will test this belief against recent studies in biology, neuroscience, and social theory. If conclusive proof is not forthcoming about us being hard-wired one way or the other, then it becomes a case of choosing which theory one feels expresses the best aspects of our nature, and making as good a case for it as possible in terms of its social effects.

Selfish Genes and Social Brains

Richard Dawkins' theory of the selfish gene has continued to be the subject of much debate since its publication in 1976. This is partly because of the title, which the author now says might better have been *The Immortal Gene*, *The Cooperative Gene*, or *The Altruistic Vehicle*, to avoid the various misinterpretations to which it has subsequently given rise.[3] In no sense is the book a defence of human selfishness, as some mistakenly have thought, and it tends to divide its readers across ideological lines. Dawkins' contention is that although each individual gene is 'pursuing its own self-interested agenda', Darwinian '[n]atural selection [. . .] sees to it that gangs of mutually compatible – which is almost to say cooperating – genes are favoured in the presence of each other'.[4] Dawkins discriminates between what happens at a micro level, the gene itself being the unit where natural selection takes place and thus being describable as selfish in striving to ensure its own survival, and macro levels such as organisms where altruism can develop. 'Kin altruism', he suggests, could be one of the ways in which 'gene selfishness can translate into individual altruism', with individual organisms 'feeding and protecting kin who are likely to share copies of the same gene'.[5] The discrepancy between the two states noted by Dawkins is reminiscent of that between the micro and macro levels of the physical world, with the randomness identified by physicists at the former level being experienced as order by us at the latter, the realm of everyday life.

Although he is at pains to insist that he is not as such arguing the case for altruism as an innate property of human beings, biology providing little evidence for this, Dawkins nevertheless thinks that it is a trait worth developing in our social existence, and he encourages us to

> discuss ways of deliberately cultivating and nurturing pure, disinterested altruism – something that has no place in nature, something that has never existed before in the whole history of the world. We are built as gene machines and cultured as meme machines, but we have the power to turn against our creators. We, alone on earth, can rebel against the tyranny of the selfish replicators.[6]

One can see why this would attract criticism from those who believe we are naturally competitive and should therefore design our society, and particularly our economic system, to fit that presumed innate property. Dawkins is saying that we can choose how we behave towards each other; 'we are', as he puts it, 'capable of rebelling against our selfish genes'.[7] Altruism is his preferred choice of social behaviour; although he does make a point of emphasising the practical benefits that can accrue from this, as in the case of 'reciprocal altruism': 'If animals live together in groups then their genes must get more benefit out of the association than they put in.'[8] That can only come across as an ideologically motivated decision to advocates of competition, however, since it is calling into question their belief that rugged individualism best expresses the human character: altruism from this perspective can appear like the first step on the road to socialism. They would much prefer it if the selfish gene dictated our character right through to the macro level to justify their conception of the free market, where competition must always be considered to reign supreme. That would be a micro–macro link of considerable ideological power.

Dawkins feels he can identify a disposition towards altruism at the macro level of organisms, and takes this as proof of our ability to override the agenda of our selfish genes. But if it really is a matter of choice then that means we could choose to go with the selfishness and not rebel against our genes, arguing that to develop this trait as much as we were able, to rebel against altruism perhaps, would be the best way to increase our resilience as a society. Excessive altruism, from this standpoint, merely holds us back and prevents us from becoming more independent beings. Either choice could be defended, and we find ourselves plunged back into an apparent ideological stalemate; so it becomes a case of examining the advantages and disadvantages involved in adopting either position to see if one can be deemed preferable to the other.

Advocates claim that competition spurs us on to improve our performance and efficiency and that where this is not present we will rest on our laurels, that unless we are continually tested in this way then we are likely to stagnate: essentially, that is James Murdoch's line about public broadcasting. This is a belief that would seem to be borne out to some degree by the findings of chaos and complexity theory, which suggest that species thrive best when they are positioned at the 'edge of chaos', being forced to exert themselves to stay on the right side of the borderline. It is a notion which has an obvious appeal to the business community, and it has attracted the interest of some business studies theorists.[9] What this does not tell us, however, is what the rewards should be for success in competition against others. Even if altruists might concede the social benefits of competition up to a point, what they find more difficult to accept is the scale of the rewards that tend to be involved. There are the huge bonuses paid out in the finance industry to be considered, for example, or the multimillion-pound annual contracts that top footballers routinely can negotiate throughout their career. These rewards have dramatically increased in recent years out of all proportion to average earnings, so one could say that one of the main effects of encouraging competition, in the largely unregulated way that neoliberals tirelessly keep campaigning for, is significantly to widen the disparities of wealth in our society. This is unlikely to do much for social cohesion, a point made very force-fully in Richard Wilkinson and Kate Pickett's book *The Spirit Level*.[10] Neither could it exactly be said that neoliberal-style competition has improved performance in banking or the finance industry in general; instead, massive rewards merely appear to have encour-aged massive risks to be taken, and then massive crashes to occur when these fail to work out as hoped.

Altruism is perhaps a rather specific concept to be using in this context, however, when it is properly speaking cooperation that is opposite to competition. Cooperation has been at the centre of social existence over the course of human history, and its virtues are very obvious: groups clearly offer greater security to the individual, whether living in permanent settlements or following the nomadic lifestyle celebrated by such as Deleuze and Guattari.[11] Cooperation is in fact one of the most important aspects of culture, and it is our heritage of this, as Dawkins keeps reminding us, that most distin-guishes us from the rest of the animal kingdom: we are 'uniquely dominated by culture, by influences learned and handed down'.[12] The value of cooperation is easy to establish, therefore, and even neoliberals are not going to argue against that; chaotic though it may be, the market is nevertheless a group activity. But the neo-liberal line would seem to be that if we put ever more emphasis on individualism and competition, then we shall move ourselves onto a higher level of social existence that will be to our benefit as a species; it is that assumption that asks to be challenged. Does market competition really improve the general lifestyle of human-kind? Or would we be better to encourage a greater degree of coop-eration instead, leading perhaps to the greater degree of economic equality argued for by Wilkinson and Pickett?

Competition is now well embedded in our notion of culture too, of course; capitalism and modernity have been based on that, it is arguably their most defining feature. Capitalist modernity can claim many successes and there is no denying that it has radically altered human existence over the last few centuries, transforming our lives particularly through the development of technology. We have routinely come to expect our standard of living to go on improving throughout the course of our lives, and although the recent financial crisis has cast doubt on our ability to go on doing this as a culture, it is still the stated objective of the main political parties throughout the West and the issue that tends to dominate in most general elections. What is ignored most of the time is the downside of capitalist cooperation globally. It is competition, in the service of the profit motive, that has sanctioned the systematic exploitation of the developing world; first of all for the raw materials needed to manufacture the products that the West desired, and then to assemble those same products more cheaply than could be done in the West itself so that prices could be driven down there to maximise sales. The more cheaply you or your company can sell your products then the greater your share of the profits to be made in your area will be, forcing your competitors to look for ways to do the same to keep pace – and all to the consumer's gain, as the system keeps telling us.

While market-led competition has undeniably led to a higher standard of living in the West, its record elsewhere is generally quite abysmal. Multinationals are driving harder and harder bargains in return for transferring their manufacturing operations to developing countries, which are obliged to keep their labour costs to a minimum to succeed in what has become a particularly cut-throat market. Western consumers gain at someone else's expense, therefore, but then it is intrinsic to the very notion of competition that there are always going to be both winners and losers, whatever the game being played. It is the discrepancy between the two that should be concerning us, however, especially when it is as stark in economic terms as it patently is in this case.

Encouraging cooperation has always been a primary concern of socialism, which tends to want to curb the competitive instinct, with its individualistic overtones, in order to achieve greater equality of treatment throughout society. The objection levelled against this by advocates of competition is that it hampers the development of initiative and entrepreneurialism, thus lowering the standard of living over time. Unfortunately enough for socialists, communism seems to offer a readily available example of how this can indeed come to pass, as neoliberals are never slow to point out. But communism is a special case, particularly in its Soviet version, and the point must always be made that the application of socialist principles need not have that effect. Where social democracy has been strong, in Scandinavia for example, living standards have kept pace with the rest of the capitalist world, while overall quality of life has arguably improved.

Dawkins' warning against not basing one's morality on the processes of evolution is always worth bearing in mind: we 'can expect little help from biological nature' if we begin such a project.[13] We are neither purely a product of nature nor of nurture; the latter can be used to modify the former so that we are, as it were, a work in progress on a terrain that includes both biology and ideology. Choosing to emphasise one side or the other, or what nurture itself should actually involve, requires a case to be made. It is over the question of what nurture should involve where this debate is at its most interesting, and that leads us right back into the arena of culture.

The RSA's Social Brain project has come to very similar conclusions about our disposition towards altruism and cooperation; indeed, it takes altruism to be one of the main qualities it wants to promote in society, the others being 'active engagement in public decision-making' and 'self-reliance'.[14] The RSA is a think tank dedicated to maintaining the legacy of the Enlightenment, and it has taken particular issue with the notion of us as self-interested, innately competitive individuals. Against this, it espouses a view of human nature that pictures us as:

- Constituted by evolutionary biology
- Embedded in complex social networks
- Largely habitual creatures

- Highly sensitive to social and cultural norms
- More rationalising than rational.[15]

These are conclusions reached on the basis of recent research in social psychology, behavioural economics, and neuroscience, and they run directly counter to prevailing neoliberal wisdom that sees us as programmed for a life of market competition and frustrated if we are not allowed to engage in this without restriction. As far as the Social Brain team are concerned, 'humans are a fundamentally social species', and once again we find the factor of culture being very strongly emphasised.[16] We are inescapably embedded in complex social networks with a long tradition behind them.

The Social Brain project's report, 'Changing the subject', sets out to construct an alternative to what it describes as the 'unrealistic and narrow view of human agency that people might hold' by bringing to our attention 'new studies on the human brain and behaviour'.[17] It is firmly opposed to the idea that we are essentially selfish creatures and wants to play up the benefits of cooperation instead. Ultimately, the goal is to bring about social change; but not of the kind that neoliberals are agitating for, even if self-reliance is to play its part in the process. It advocates developing social institutions that preserve our personal autonomy yet enable us also to engage fruitfully in collective action; if we can do so then we will have achieved 'a synthesis of conservative and social-democratic thinking' that 'will have a very broad appeal'.[18] That notion is heavily based on the 'Third Way' theories put forward by Anthony Giddens in the 1990s, and which were so influential in New Labour thinking throughout its time in government, 1997–2010.[19]

It is perhaps difficult now to detach Giddens' Third Way from New Labour, whose interpretation of the idea is open to a lot of criticism. New Labour very consciously set out to distance themselves from the paternalistic, anti-business image they were associated with, the party of nationalisation and high taxes, and tried their best to come to an accommodation with the business world, particularly its financial side; hence Peter Mandelson's remark about the party being relaxed about the rich becoming ever richer under the new regime. In common with most governments throughout the West, New Labour worked to loosen regulations on the finance industry, seeing this as the key to creating an era of national economic prosperity, this time to be based on service industries rather than manufacturing. An economic boom duly followed and the City of London was seen as central to maintaining this in its provision of income-generating financial services, leading to quite a cosy relationship developing between the government and the finance community: Gordon Brown, in his role as Chancellor of the Exchequer, going out of his way to compliment the City's efforts on several occasions.

It could be argued that in retrospect New Labour drifted more towards the right-wing end of the Third Way spectrum than to the left or even centre ground, especially when it came to its economic policy, which was in the main fairly libertarian in character, more concerned overall with wealth creation than wealth distribution. That is how the report views it, arguing that New Labour was unduly influenced by Friedmanite theory during its time in office to the detriment of its traditional socio-political ideals. Perhaps the Third Way does not need to work out like that, with the rich becoming progressively richer and the income disparities ever more pronounced, but it is how it is most likely to be perceived for the immediate future in the popular consciousness. The question will always arise in such a system as to how much latitude should be given to the forces of profit, and that is why 'Changing the subject' lays greater stress on institutions than there has been in recent political history, criticising New Labour for a failure to develop these to any significant extent as a bulwark against socially divisive neoliberal practices.

The report emphasises that socialism and neoliberalism do have features in common, such as a persistent belief 'that people can form perfect social systems'.[20] For the former it is the state-controlled and directed application of science and technology that ultimately will achieve this; while for the latter it is the workings of the market, which has been neatly dubbed a 'marketopian' outlook.[21] Taking its cue from Giddens, an advocate of 'methodical doubt' about our beliefs in general, the report recommends treating the notion of human perfectibility with a fair degree of scepticism, arguing that this is a deeply flawed idea that simply does not acknowledge the full complexity of human desires and social interactions.[22] Postmodern theory has taken a similar line on human nature, emphasising the differences between individuals and also between cultures, and insisting that we can never exercise complete control over others or the environment. There is a general sense of scepticism about such theory which I very much wish to endorse as a trait worth developing in our political discourse, although it does not rule out the possibility of improving the quality of life and human relations in general.[23]

The report concludes that the Third Way notion still has mileage if it can recapture its early ideals: 'In terms of contemporary British politics, there does seem to be a move towards a real Third Way – one where "one nation" conservatism is melded with progressive commitments.'[24] The Social Brain team want to build on that general desire, and it is to recent brain research, neuroscience, and the concept of neurological reflexivity, that they turn in order to provide a more scientific basis for a Third Way politics than Giddens did; neuroscience having the considerable benefit of being 'about something very personal and therefore graspable by all of us'.[25] Neuroscience, they argue, provides hard evidence of the value of our existing social institutions in promoting social solidarity, as well as of the need to create effective new ones that 'work with and not against the grain of human nature'.[26] It will only be through the work of such institutions that we shall find ourselves able to overcome the limitations of our brain processes, since, no matter what we might think, we are not very good at long-term planning as individuals. As the report notes, we are far more likely at individual level to gravitate towards whatever offers us immediate gratification, rationalisation winning out over rationality; it is only through our social side that we can overcome this trait.

Neuroscience posits two major systems at work in the human brain: the automatic brain and the controlled brain. These are in constant interaction with each other, and the critical point to be borne in mind is the essential plasticity of the brain, which means it is able to change and develop over time. We are not, as neoliberals hold, 'isolated and self-interested individuals who band together in order to better enjoy the fruits of their labour', but intrinsically social animals deeply interested in each other.[27] Neoliberalism does seem to underestimate our social needs quite drastically, regarding society as little better than a necessary evil, an evil that must be kept to a minimum in terms of its institutions and power to intervene in our lives – and especially in the market. This is a model of social existence that the Social Brain team rejects, and the polemical side of the project comes through very forcefully in assertions like the following:

> [T]he self as an isolated and disembodied decision-maker in total control of behaviour would seem to be a fiction. A large portion of our behaviour seems to result from automatic reactions to the social situations we are in, as well as a concern to abide by social norms.[28]

Neoliberals, of course, base their conception of the market on such rational decision-making processes being entirely natural to us, and that these are geared to maximising individual self-interest wherever possible. Altruism would simply hinder the working of those processes and is therefore to be avoided: to succumb to it would almost be a sign of character weakness since your competitors would undoubtedly take advantage of it at your expense. For the Social Brain project, however, altruism is a source of feelings of well-being, as several studies have concluded, and this clearly has significant social benefits. The message of the Social Brain team is that we can entrench this trait more firmly within our social existence by developing institutions that actively encourage its expression: 'as a society we should think seriously about how we can create the conditions where it is the norm to be altruistic.'[29]

Neuroscience seems to reveal that we can to some extent draw on our biological nature to construct our moral codes, but that such nature has to be nurtured in order to bring it out, otherwise it may just remain latent in us. As far as the Social Brain project is concerned, it is never a case of nature or nurture when trying to work out the driver behind human behaviour; that is a false division since the two are always interacting with each other and modifying each other's characteristics. That does raise the possibility, however, that one could adapt neuroscientific findings to a neoliberal agenda by nurturing the traits you want and simply ignoring those that you do not. There is evidence to suggest that if our disposition towards altruism and social relationships is not nurtured when we are young then we tend to develop into emotionally cold and unsympathetic beings in adulthood. That is not likely to be too many people's choice of character, and it is not the Social Brain team's. Yet the point does stand that it is a matter of choice what traits we do develop in human beings, that we might choose to suppress our altruistic potential in favour of our competitive if that leads to the kind of society we've decided we want – a neoliberal, market-oriented one, for example. In real terms, that is what many of us have probably already done, and the Social Brain team is acutely aware of 'the possibility that people will tell us they simply don't care about this new knowledge'.[30] Profit has such a powerful grip on our culture at the moment that this may well happen. But as the project also goes on to insist, if we react in that way then we shall be unable to find solutions to the many problems that collectively we face at present, such as the credit crisis and global warming. These are problems, it should be remembered, stemming largely from the assumption that we are above all self-interested competitive individuals who can only realise our true nature in a market economy setting. At the very least, greater awareness of neurological reflexivity should help to stimulate debate about such pressing issues, and the potential of a 'real Third Way' deserves to be explored further – even if neither the extreme right nor the extreme left will see any need to do so, being locked into their respective dogmas and not much inclined towards compromise. Something else both sides would seem to share is a belief that 'there is no alternative'.

Trade unionism would seem to provide evidence for the Social Brain, in that it represents a reaction to the cult of individualism and the belief that our own self-interest is all that counts, the primary motivation in our dealings with others. What trade union membership offers instead is a sense of solidarity and unity that encourages us to put the collective interest first. Anyone who has ever been a member of a trade union will know how powerful that sense of solidarity can be and how much less vulnerable it can make one feel as an individual up against the superior force of management. It is no accident that one of the main concerns of neoliberalism since it became an economic paradigm has been to break the powers of trade unions. Neoliberals much prefer an atomised workforce where individuals have to compete against each other for whatever rewards are available, as determined by the market. Trade union membership has in fact declined in the West in recent decades, and neoliberals have contrived to find more and more ways to make the work contract less secure such that there is less concerted opposition to the application of their doctrines. Short-term and part-time contracts have become much more common across the employment spectrum, and these hardly encourage challenging management about its practices.

Another neuroscience-influenced thinker to emphasise cultural tradition is David Brooks, whose book *The Social Animal*, a novel of ideas, is attracting a great deal of attention at the moment on both sides of the Atlantic.[31] The book has made a big impression on the political class in America and the UK, particularly amongst those on the right who see it as providing arguments to bolster the 'Big Society' notion. Brooks takes issue with the cult of reason that treats us as rational machines only concerned with maximising our own self-interest, and recommends that we should follow our emotional intuitions more. His ideas hark back to eighteenth-century thinkers like Edmund Burke and David Hume, the former an important influence on the older style of conservatism that the right, especially in the UK, tended to espouse before neoliberal-inspired neoconservatism largely supplanted it.

Brooks is quite taken by the idea of the Big Society, and this has endeared him to the UK's Conservative Party, although he has expressed reservations about the way the coalition government is currently going about implementing it, asserting in an interview that, '[w]hat I want to say to David Cameron is that if you decentral-

ise power you risk getting rid of a basic level of fairness and equality. And you risk creating separate communities that don't talk to
each other.'[32] In other words, long-established institutions still have
a critical role to play in our lives and must not be summarily abol-
ished for purely ideological reasons; with the qualification that they
really must be based on principles of fairness and equality rather
than just tradition for its own sake. It is questionable, for example,
whether aristocracy, the monarchy, or the House of Lords, are really
necessary in order for us to realise our status as social animals or to
satisfy the promptings of our social brain. The left, the big defenders
of social institutions, would mostly demur on such cases as these,
arguing that only institutions directly concerned with protecting
the welfare of the mass should count.

What the Big Society claims to be and what it is proving to be
in reality are, therefore, not necessarily the same thing. If the Big
Society continues to be essentially a tax-cutting exercise hiding
behind some fairly empty communitarian rhetoric, then separate
communities is precisely what we shall find ourselves landed with.
We are well on the way to that state already after several decades of
neoliberalism. Neoliberalism is about the self-interested animal not
the social one, and we have to treat it as suspicious if it ever claims
to be the route to a more communitarian future. The only interest
neoliberals have in communities is if they buy things to increase
their profit margins; it is only if they do that, and cost no money in
terms of public services in order to enable them to be consumers,
that they will be tolerated.

Science aside, the message that comes through loud and clear in
both Dawkins and the Social Brain project is that we are above all
products of culture, and that culture can always be modified. We
might not be able to escape the past but we can always reinterpret
it. Neither can we change the basics of our biological nature, but we
can choose which aspects of it to emphasise. The drive to pursue
profit is not encoded in our genes, therefore, yet that fact alone does
not tell us what form of society to develop; that is always going to
be a matter for negotiation.

6

Neoliberalism, Financial Crisis, and Profit

For the next five chapters I will be exploring neoliberalism and its role in Western culture in greater detail; the intention being to try and work out why it is that its advocates are so keen to extend its sphere of influence, and, equally, why we should resist their determined efforts to do so. Just what is the hold that neoliberalism exercises over us, and why its obsession with profit? Until we start asking questions like this we remain at the mercy of the neoliberal juggernaut and its domination of the political sphere. As Susan George has so neatly summed it up: 'Over the past three decades, the monetary economy has taken over, neglected the real economy and become virtually separate from it, while the real economy itself increasingly serves the needs of a minority.'[1] Neoliberalism has been all about the monetary economy, not the real economy of trade and manufacture, and the monetary economy has been all about profit: profit now, with no thought for others or the future. John Lanchester's take on Iceland's economic collapse in the wake of the credit crisis was that, 'basically a small group of rich and powerful people sold assets back and forwards to each other and created a grotesque bubble of phoney wealth', an assessment that can be applied more generally to the global financial community operating in its own self-contained economy, oblivious to the needs of the outside world.[2] How that minority has managed to bend us to its will, to change democracy into profitocracy, I'll now consider.

70

We now have a dramatic example of what happens when we give the profit motive more or less free rein to operate in the market – the recent financial crisis, which still hangs over us several years after it first broke, and continues to baffle our political class who had been assuming that such setbacks would only ever be temporary from now on, mere blips in an inexorable onward progress to ever-improving living standards for everyone. The financial industry was actively encouraged by the majority of governments in the West to pursue profit at the expense of almost all other considerations, with legislation being systematically relaxed on the industry's dealings to give them more room for manoeuvre. Greed was being given official approval as the way to economic prosperity, with the dire consequences that we have all since witnessed, and indeed are still witnessing in the form of government spending cutbacks on the large scale and a general shift of what were hitherto public services into the private sector. All this plus a relentless campaign by the right to make public service in general seem right at the root of our economic problems and thus ripe for 'reform'.

Nevertheless, the response of the majority of the political class in the West has been to reiterate its faith in neoliberal economics and the market fundamentalist ethos, contenting itself with, at best, a bit of tweaking to the system here and there in the hope that this will prevent more financial bubbles from occurring, or at least make them less catastrophic in scale than the one we have just experienced. Even more worryingly, most of the population seems ready to go along with this policy decision, and, with either good or bad grace, depending on your political persuasion, to accept that substantial cuts in public services are the necessary price to be paid for keeping a profit-obsessed system going.

Another government initiative designed to foster an alternative to the public sector has been to encourage the development of employee-run and owned mutual societies. Such organisations as the highly regarded department store chain John Lewis are put forward as models of how these could be run, with employees turning into shareholders and thus having a personal interest in the group's performance. Mutuals formed in what is currently the public sector would then be in a position to negotiate contracts with elected bodies to deliver the services they needed, and a few schemes of this nature are already under way in the UK. This has the advantage of making the government look as if it is taking the welfare of the populace seriously, and genuinely searching for new ways to safeguard this; but there will always be a doubt as to how such groups will function in the long term in competition with other more market-oriented providers. Mutualism appears to be an example of cooperation in action, but business considerations, and the lure of profit, could well come in time to dominate and undermine the public-spirited motives that led to the societies' formation. What would happen, for example, if mutuals were thrown into serious, and even cut-throat, competition with each other in a declining market where the actual survival of the organisation was at stake if it did not obtain the desired contracts? Profit has a way of altering people's ethics, and as one commentator has suggested, mutual societies could well 'turn out to be sinister Trojan horses' doing neoliberalism's dirty work for it, leaving welfare provision in the hands of publicly unaccountable bodies.[3]

The World According to Neoliberalism

I'll now survey the development of neoliberalism, from the theories of Adam Smith through such modern luminaries as Friedrich Hayek and Milton Friedman, to determine what Western politicians such as Margaret Thatcher and Ronald Reagan and so many of their successors, including the current coalition government in the UK, have taken from them. So enthusiastic has been the reception of neoliberalism by such politicians as the above that it has had the effect of marginalising the more public-spirited economic theories of John Maynard Keynes, which had been widely adopted from the Great Depression onwards. President Franklin D. Roosevelt's 'New Deal' programme, for example, with its strong commitment to public works as a method of kick-starting a stagnant economy, was an essentially Keynesian exercise.[4]

Not that neoliberalism is without its critics. The robust criticisms offered to its economic schemes by such recent commentators as David Harvey, John Gray, John Holloway, and Naomi Klein – and even by those broadly in favour of it such as Joseph Stiglitz – will be noted, and the earlier objections to capitalism put forward by Karl Marx still resonate in this context.[5] But it is striking how even Marx has been appropriated by the neoliberals in recent years, as if all such criticism is merely a misunderstanding of what a neoliberal economic world offers humanity, and that once this is cleared up then the neoliberal case becomes unanswerable. So it becomes a case of: Marx, great analyst but poor prophet. Even the credit crisis does not seem to have altered the triumphalist attitudes of the neoliberal camp, although it is interesting to note that the concept of 'de-growth' is now beginning to attract more attention amongst economists, suggesting that dissent from the paradigm is there to be built on. The work of Serge Latouche is particularly thought-provoking on that latter point, and I will be returning to it later in the chapter.[6]

Overall, however, neoliberalism is still what drives economic thinking in most Western governmental circles, and as the following chapters go on to show, that is having some disastrous effects on the public sector, and even more crucially, on the planet's ecosystem: profit may well turn out to be the human race's greatest folly. Neoliberalism is not just an economic theory, it's a creed; in Charles R. Morris's well-chosen phrase, it 'has mutated from a style of analysis into a Theory of Everything'.[7] So we need to keep undermining its belief system, pointing up its manifold contradictions and inconsistencies, if we are to prevent ourselves from being led ever deeper into that folly. As postmodern theory keeps reminding us, theories of everything in the socio-political realm in reality amount to theories of how to exert power over others.

Adam Smith is revered by neoliberals, who treat him as the founder of modern economics and quote him the way the far left so often quotes Marx: as if the mere recital of his thoughts was enough to end any argument about how to run the economy. The concept of the 'invisible hand' is trotted out at every opportunity and is considered the most powerful rebuttal to the notion of a centrally planned economy by its apparent championship of the entrepreneur:

> He generally, indeed, neither intends to promote the publick interest, nor knows how much he is promoting it. By preferring the support of domestick to that of foreign industry, he intends only his own security; and by directing that industry in such a manner as its produce may be of the greatest value, he intends only his own gain, and he is in this, as in many other cases, led by an invisible hand to promote an end which was no part of his intention.[8]

What is usually ignored by neoliberals, however, is the historical context within which Smith was working and thus his particular reasons for developing his theories. Economic life at the time in the eighteenth century was heavily dominated by monopolies, and Smith was aware that collectively these constituted a considerable block on economic development. The free market, with its internally operative 'invisible hand' as a regulating mechanism to a much more open, less autocratically controlled system, was put forward by Smith as an alternative to monopolies, and by the standards of the era it was a progressive idea. In theory, it opened up the market to anyone with the requisite ambition, and not just the rich and well-connected: it was a democratising notion for a culture which was still lacking such staples of democracy as a universal franchise. What that does not mean, however, is that it remains a progressive idea for all times and all societies, regardless of how much the historical context may have changed in the interim. We might also wonder, too, what neoliberals make of Smith's defence of 'domestick' against 'foreign' industry, which hardly provides support for the globalisation ethic.

What is also rarely noted by neoliberals is that Smith does not lay all that much emphasis on the invisible hand; in fact it only puts in one appearance over the course of his magnum opus, *An Enquiry into the Wealth of Nations*, meaning that one has to conjecture what those 'many other cases' mentioned in the quote above might involve. And as Susan George has noted of the work, it has 'been used to justify all manner of mischief and any number of practices Smith would have decried, particularly in his other well-known work, *The Theory of Moral Sentiments*'.[9] In the latter work, we find Smith at pains to emphasise virtue and morality over mere wealth and the personal power it confers:

> The disposition to admire, and almost to worship, the rich and power-ful, and to despise, or, at least, to neglect persons of poor and mean con-dition, though necessary both to establish the distinction of ranks and the order of society, is, at the same time, the great and most universal cause of the corruption of our moral sentiments.[10]

This hardly sounds like the champion of rugged individualism that Smith has been turned into by neoliberals; the inspiration for think-tanks like the Adam Smith Institute, for example. Nor does he sound as rabid an advocate of self-interest as they claim either when we consider sentiments like the following:

> How selfish soever man may be supposed, there are evidently some principles in his nature, which interest him in the fortune of others, and render their happiness necessary to him, though he derives nothing from it except the pleasure of seeing it. Of this kind is pity or compas-sion, the emotion which we feel for the misery of others, when we either see it, or are made to conceive it in a very lively manner. [. . .] The greatest ruffian, the most hardened violator of the laws of society, is not altogether without it.[11]

It would be stretching a point to interpret this as a manifesto for the development of a profitocracy, which encourages a much narrower vision of social relations based on competitive feelings rather than sympathy towards others. What neoliberalism seems to give us is not just Smith without the history, but Smith without the morality.

The title of one of Hayek's most influential books, *The Road to Serfdom*, makes it clear how dangerous he feels the idea of a planned society on the socialist model is. Socialism is to be avoided at all costs for this thinker, and his admirers have continued to propound that doctrine into the twenty-first century. Hayek believes that the concept of freedom has been grossly distorted by socialism, and that its claims to lead to this for the mass of the population are misleading:

> There can be no doubt that the promise of greater freedom has become one of the most effective weapons of socialist propaganda and that the belief that socialism would bring freedom is genuine and sincere. But this would only heighten the tragedy if it should prove that what was promised to us as the Road to Freedom was in fact the High Road to Servitude.[12]

And that is exactly what socialism has become in Hayek's reading of world history, a full-blown tragedy that has reduced rather than increased our level of personal freedom. Allowances must be made for the fact that he was writing during the Second World War when socialism was most identified in the public mind with National Socialism and Soviet communism, both of them strongly reliant on the concept of collectivism with all its overtones of coercion and loss of personal identity. Yet Hayek did not change his mind substantially when more benign versions of socialism in the guise of social democracy took shape throughout Western Europe in the postwar era, as they did in the UK and Scandinavia, for example. In the preface to the 1976 edition of the book, he concedes that these are less doctrinaire, but nevertheless insists that 'the ultimate outcome tends to be very much the same'.[13]

Socialist planning has the effect of removing competition from economic life. Hayek finds that unacceptable, working instead on 'the conviction that where effective competition can be created, it is a better way of guiding individual efforts than any other', and that this is 'the only method by which our activities can be adjusted to each other without coercive or arbitrary intervention of authority'.[14] It is to be considered 'the price of democracy' that 'in some fields things must be left to chance', and as central planning almost completely precludes this from occurring, it is to be avoided.[15] Although there is a nod to what became the social democratic model of the state when Hayek comments that welfare services need not be seen as incompatible with a socio-economic system structured on competition, what that has come to mean under neoliberal pressure in our own time is that there has to be competition within the actual welfare services themselves, which are then opened up to the private sector – a change which has altered the perspective on what welfare is actually about. For socialists, welfare traditionally has been a method of redistributing wealth, but competition has come to mean keeping costs down and removing recipients wherever possible; the argument being that too much welfare leads to a state of dependency that is not in the tax-paying public's interest to maintain. To this end, the UK's coalition government is currently conducting a high-profile public campaign to cut down on this supposed dependency, the argument being that this will help turn the UK into a more economically competitive society: welfare in general comes out of such an exercise with its reputation severely tainted.

Hayek is a fervent supporter of nineteenth-century liberalism, which along with the doctrines of Adam Smith, although a highly selective reading of these as we have seen, constitute the main source of the neoliberal ethic. *The Road to Serfdom* is in many ways a paean to this tradition:

> Though we neither can wish, nor possess the power, to go back to the reality of the nineteenth century, we have the opportunity to realise its ideals – and they were not mean. [. . .] The guiding principle, that a policy of freedom for the individual is the only truly progressive policy, remains as true to-day as it was in the nineteenth century.[16]

Neoliberals are enthusiastically carrying on that programme into the twenty-first century, although it is yet another highly idealistic view of the past that is involved here – certainly not a nineteenth century that Karl Marx for one would recognise. Freedom can indeed mean many things, and market freedom and freedom from economic exploitation are simply incompatible: we find ourselves standing at the fault line between neoliberalism and socialism at such points.

Friedman, too, is an uncompromising critic of socialist doctrines and the collectivist ethic, which he sees as running counter to the

American way of life and its commitment to a rugged individualism, as well as ingrained suspicion of big government: the 'frontier' spirit that still lingers in the national consciousness and informs so much of its worldview. It is a case of the less government the better for this thinker, whose ideas have been massively influential in shaping the politics of such figures as Ronald Reagan and Margaret Thatcher. Neoliberal ideology owes much to Friedman, with powerful bodies such as the IMF and World Bank following a conspicuously Friedmanite line when dealing with the world's debtor countries, insisting that they slash their public sector and put their faith in free enterprise in order to resurrect their ailing economies.

Friedman was adamant that private enterprise was what we should be relying on to drive our societies, and that voluntary cooperation generally constituted enough of a check on its activities to prevent significant abuses from occurring. Other than maintaining law and order, he saw little need for government to be involved very much at all in our everyday affairs – and certainly not in the affairs of the business world, past setting some very basic parameters for company conduct. Once the market was up and running, governments were expected to stay out of the way and leave the system to develop naturally, leaving the invisible hand to do its work.

Political freedom is inseparable from the free market for Friedman, sentiments that James Murdoch fully shares. A firm opponent of government-run welfare schemes of any type, Friedman declared himself implacably opposed to socialism: 'a society which is socialist cannot also be democratic'.[17] Even to suggest that a business should have a 'social conscience' was to Friedman tantamount to 'preaching pure and unadulterated socialism', and thus 'undermining the basis of a free society'.[18] Friedman's line was that when businesses chose to act for the public good rather than the interests of their shareholders, then they were using those shareholders' money illicitly: 'in effect imposing taxes, on the one hand, and deciding how the tax proceeds shall be spent, on the other'.[19] A breach of the shareholders' rights was taking place, in this instance their right as individuals to decide what to do with their own money – one of humanity's most basic rights in Friedman's worldview. Corporate executives are in post purely to serve the shareholders' interest, which for Friedman can only mean their desire to make as much profit on their investment as possible. Friedman does not rule out the possibility of altruistic actions, but insists that they are the province of individuals not corporations; for the latter, profit must always come first:

> [T]here is one and only one social responsibility of business – to use its resources and engage in activities designed to increase its profits so long as it stays within the rules of the game, which is to say, engages in open and free competition without deception or fraud.[20]

From such a perspective the pursuit of profit is the pursuit of democratic freedom, anything at all that hinders this counts as socialism, and socialism is therefore the enemy of true democracy: true democracy really is envisaged as a profitocracy. The very concept of taxation comes to seem problematical, verging on a misuse of others' money: hence the consistent neoliberal arguments about the need to keep this low by curtailing the scope of the public sector.

Despite the link made between the market and freedom, Friedman essentially seems to regard the world of business as separate from the rest of our lives. We can do whatever we want in the latter realm, even be altruistic if we like, or have a social conscience and follow up its dictates, but we should not take any of those feelings into the former. It is as if they were self-contained areas, the only link being that if we don't have the market then we cannot expect to have freedom. Social responsibility, Friedman insists, is something that belongs to individuals not to corporations anyway: 'A corporation is an artificial person and in this sense may have artificial responsibilities, but "business" as a whole cannot be said to have responsibilities.'[21] The only way we should ever express social responsibility is in our private lives, using our own private resources, and neoliberals have no objection to this because in such cases we are 'acting as a principal, not an agent'.[22] Friedman is uncompromising on this issue, arguing that to decide to pursue social responsibility within a corporation, in the guise of, say, an executive, is to act against the interest of our employers. That interest can only ever be profit, profit, and yet more profit. Corporations have no other social role than to provide us with work and an entry into the market, so the idea of nationalisation to make key industries more socially responsible is totally unacceptable to the neoliberal mind.

Being an artificial person clears the way to concentrate on the market to the exclusion of all else. To act in any other way is, Friedman believes, to misuse your employer's time and money, and of course those of the shareholders too, and thus to be considered as 'approaching fraud':[23] it could hardly be put more provocatively than that. The condition of artificiality also appears to absolve those involved of all moral responsibility except to follow the laws of the land to the letter, and as far as Friedman and his ilk are concerned, to keep on lobbying politicians to make these as business-friendly as possible, with low taxation on both personal and corporate income. And Friedman really does mean 'to the letter', as he frowns on companies that go further than the law requires them to do in activities like fighting pollution; again, that is to waste profits which rightly should be pocketed by owners and shareholders.

It was such uncompromising views as these that proceeded to endear Friedman not just to Ronald Reagan and Margaret Thatcher, inveterate anti-socialists both, but to a succession of hard-line right-wing regimes in South America who, under IMF and World Bank prompting, adopted his ideas in the closing decades of the twentieth century in what is now widely considered to have been a disastrous socio-economic experiment that created turmoil within their respective countries that resonates through to this day. If market freedom applied in the latter cases, political freedom as we understand it in the West manifestly did not. Socialists were not merely criticised by the regime, they were branded enemies of the state throughout South America and imprisoned and even murdered for their beliefs: 'disappeared', in the euphemism employed at the time. Socialism was regarded as equivalent to sedition, and treated accordingly. Yet Margaret Thatcher could regard Chile's autocratic ruler General Pinochet, later to be pursued for crimes against humanity by the International Court of Justice at The Hague, as a kindred soul, and even allow him to reside in the UK as a political refugee when he was eventually forced to flee his home country.

We are still hearing the argument that big government is bad government in the aftermath of the Reagan–Thatcher era, and the 'Big Society' notion is merely the latest attempt to give Friedmanite doctrine a more human face than that era tended to; 'compassionate conservatism' being an earlier shot at this by George W. Bush when he was governor of Texas, and a carefully cultivated part of his public image in his campaign for the presidency. Behind this shift of focus lies the idea that taxes are somehow immoral, and that to lower them is to increase society's freedom. In both the cases just mentioned, the need for a welfare system to take care of society's less fortunate members is being admitted, but the responsibility for this is shifted as much as possible to the private sector, as if government involvement would only distort the ideals of such a project. The line of argument is that government involvement actually inhibits the development of compassion for others within the general populace, and reduces our concern for the less fortunate. We tend to assume that it is government's responsibility and that we can just leave it to them without any conscious input on our part. In the Big Society model such compassion and concern is deemed to find a more appropriate channel for expression through the work of voluntary organisations. The benefit for government is that such a system brings down public spending quite markedly, which can always be made to sound like a virtue when reporting back to the electorate. Yet the issue that always arises is how accountability can be guaranteed with such self-selecting bodies, which may well have their own particular ideological agenda to pursue. This could be a religious agenda, for example, as compassionate conservatism soon discovered when church-led charities put themselves forward to take over welfare schemes. The spectre of discrimination against those who do not share your belief system raises its head, and that is hardly consistent with the spirit of welfare as we have come to understand it in modern times.

Critics, however, have put forward some very serious objections to neoliberalism's claim to be of benefit to us all, to be the ideal economic system for an advanced society like ours, particularly in its

championship of a 'hands-off' approach to the market by government. David Harvey is one of the most trenchant of these critics and
he offers a Marxist-influenced perspective on neoliberal hegemony
in *A Brief History of Neoliberalism*, taking issue with the doctrine's
'pervasive effects on ways of thought to the point where it has
become incorporated into the common-sense way many of us interpret, live in, and understand the world'.[24] Harvey notes how clever
neoliberal thought has been to present itself as the champion of
'freedom', since this is a concept that pretty well anyone in the West
will agree with as a social objective, and that also resonates very
powerfully throughout the rest of the world, particularly where the
desire for democracy is being suppressed by tyrannical regimes. As
he goes on to observe, however, freedom under neoliberalism has
come to mean mainly freedom in the market, which has been to the
benefit of some much more than others in that it has 'restored power
to a narrowly defined capitalist class', leaving us much in the way
we were in Marx's time.[25] The corporate sector may have flourished
under a neoliberal regime, with its systematic programme of dereg-
ulation of free markets from state intervention, but for the majority
of us that kind of freedom is an empty concept. For all its apparent
support of individualism, the actions of the neoliberal state leave us
progressively more at the mercy of corporate power as individuals,
since in the final analysis such states 'typically favour the integrity
of the financial system and the solvency of financial institutions over
the well-being of the population or environmental quality'.[26] As the
political theorist Ulrich Beck has summed it up: 'Individualisation
means market dependency in all dimensions of living' and that
'delivers people over to an *external control and standardization* that
was unknown in the enclaves of familial and feudal subcultures'.[27]
The open markets of neoliberalism give rise to a fairly ruthless
form of competition, and that in its turn has a distinct tendency to
favour the larger corporations, which can become quite monopolis-
tic under such a regime, leaving the individual even more at their
mercy: again, this sounds like a reversion to the economic world of
the nineteenth century.

Harvey was writing in 2005 before the credit crisis struck and that event proceeded to pose some problems for neoliberalism that it probably did not think it would ever have to face. Yes, it is true that its theorists are far more interested in the integrity of the market than in our general well-being; in fact, they generally assume that the latter will follow on from the former. But the crisis meant that the only way the integrity of the market could be saved in 2007 was by governments intervening in it, and intervening to an unprecedented degree, buying up banks wholesale to prevent a global economic collapse. That was an action that ran directly counter to neoliberalism's core belief, which is to let the market alone decide which companies deserve to survive and which do not, and it should have raised more doubts about the viability of the theory than in retrospect it has done. Are we now supposed to regard the state as the last resort when things go wrong and the invisible hand fails to perform its correcting role? Western governments collectively decided that the state had to be just that in 2007, so we are surely entitled to ask why it cannot intervene in other ways to prevent our economies from sliding into a condition of last resort requiring such drastic remedial action to be taken. Or should the state stand idly by the next time a crisis on this scale occurs, as neoliberalism apparently wants it to, and allow organisations like banks simply to fail, let the social consequences be what they may? That would constitute a purist reaction to the work of the invisible hand of the market, accepting whatever it led to even if that meant wholesale economic collapse. Plainly, neoliberalism has some serious gaps as an economic theory, but as Harvey indicated, its effect on our general way of thought has been pervasive and it is reasserting itself yet again, repeating much the same doctrines as before without recognising the irony of doing so. One wonders quite what would have to happen to shake neoliberals' faith in the omnipotence of the market.

Harvey is also keen to draw our attention to the contradictions involved in neoliberalism, particularly the 'contradiction [that] arises between a seductive but alienating possessive individualism on the one hand and the desire for a meaningful collective life on the other'.[28] If anything could be said to have brought that contradiction to the forefront of the public consciousness it would have to be the credit crisis, which came very close to destroying the basis for that collective life as we currently understand it. Possessive individualism has regained the initiative since then and is doing its utmost to undermine the institutions that have been built up over time to promote meaningful collective life: it is not so much a case of there being tension between the two positions as a state of war. Rather presciently, Harvey speculates that,

> a global financial crisis in part provoked by its own reckless economic policies would permit the US government to finally rid itself of any obligation whatsoever to provide for the welfare of its citizens except for the ratcheting up of that military and police power that might be needed to quell social unrest and compel global discipline.[29]

If this complete withdrawal from welfare provision has not happened there yet under the Democrat administration that took power in 2008, it would have to be a serious possibility were there to be a Republican win next time around. It very neatly seems to sum up the ideology that is driving coalition government policy in the UK at the moment. The government is striving to divest itself of as much of the welfare state as it feels it can get away with, by threatening us with the dire consequences if we do not: the UK as the next Ireland, Greece, etc. In this context it is interesting to note the comment made by a coalition minister in defence of this policy, that '[c]ivil society has a very valuable role to play in delivering public services', with its implication that civil society is somehow completely separated from national politics.[30] The notion that national politics is in fact an expression of civil society and that the actions of national politicians are undertaken on behalf of that same society, just does not seem to impinge on the neoliberal mind. If, as Harvey was claiming in 2005, we should consider neoliberalism to be 'on trial', then it would have to be said that it is not being prosecuted anything like vigorously enough as yet.[31]

Harvey's more recent work, post-credit crisis, goes on to investigate what happens when capitalism does fail, his concern being that what we are being offered by most policy-makers in the aftermath of this particular failure is simply 'a botched return to the sort of capitalism that got us into the mess in the first place'.[32] Capitalism, he admits, is perfectly capable of recovering from this mess, but we do have to wonder 'at what cost?'.[33] Harvey is quite clear that this cost will fall disproportionately on the world's population, and that there will be, for example, an increasing investment by corporations and the finance industry in the non-Western world that will involve ever more exploitation of both the workers and the environment there. That alone may not be enough to revive the system however, and capitalism will do its best to open up new fields to generate the large profit margins it craves, such as biomedical and genetic engineering. As Harvey notes: 'The rents on intellectual property rights and patents will guarantee returns long into the future to those who hold them. (Imagine what will happen when life itself is patented!)'[34] The objective will always be profit in the shortest possible term, by whatever route promises it.

For Harvey, the overall cost is totally unacceptable, and he wants us to consider the possibility of a reformed communism as the way to avoid being caught in its toils, while being well aware of the difficulties of overcoming communism's almost universally poor public image given its largely disastrous twentieth-century history. His suggestion is that, '[p]erhaps we should just define the movement, our movement, as anti-capitalist or call ourselves the Party of Indignation, ready to fight and defeat the Party of Wall Street and its acolytes and apologists everywhere, and leave it at that.'[35] Harvey believes that we have reached 'an inflexion point in the history of capitalism' that enables such a movement to set about seriously questioning the viability of capitalism as a system, although as yet that debate has scarcely begun.[36] It is an unashamedly Marxist reading of the situation, but one that will make an impression even on those who are sceptical of the virtues of communism as a socio-economic system; certainly, there is a lot of indignation around at the moment that is just asking to be built on.

Drawing on an Edgar Allan Poe story, John Holloway likens our current situation vis-à-vis our economic system to being in a room as the walls gradually close in on us, and suggests that we seek out 'cracks' in the wall and go to work on these weak points. Further, we should strive our utmost 'to create cracks that defy the apparently unstoppable advance of capital, of the walls that are pushing us to our destruction'.[37] Holloway feels that it is a matter of exploiting the many contradictions in capitalism in order to establish new forms of social relations outside the capitalist model. Being excluded from the capitalist machine through unemployment, for example, creates the opportunity to develop such relations that 'can easily become the material basis for a sort of flip-over, a real *détournement* in which victims emerge as rebels'.[38] The extent to which that would actually occur may be debatable, but the exhortation to resist from the grass roots upwards is a powerful one.

Crack Capitalism is only too apposite a description of the current system in another way: capitalism is as addictive as a drug like 'crack', and its addicts are just as hooked on instant excitement, wanting profit now and not being overly concerned about the long-term effects of their addiction. If this were a problem only to the people most addicted, those who have chosen the lifestyle such as financial market traders, bankers, and venture capitalists, that would be fine; the rest of us could just stay clear, and take warning from observing how the addiction could distort your life and sense of proportion. Confessional tales of life in the City outline how trying to keep up with the relentless search for 'alpha' profit can reduce its participants to a quite desperate condition, both physically and psychologically; giving us a sort of *Pilgrim's Progress* of the financial life.[39] We might even feel some sympathy for those who have finally seen the light and stepped away from the madness, but the after-effects of their actions reverberate throughout all of global society. All of us are now suffering from the 'surfeit of the spirit of capitalism' such characters have left behind them:[40] addiction to capitalism is bad for everyone's health, not just that of the addicts.

Joseph Stiglitz, as befits someone who is an ex-Chief Economist and senior Vice-President of the World Bank, is a supporter of the market and of globalisation, but he believes that we are not currently going about the latter in the right way and that social fairness is signally missing; hence globalisation's many 'discontents', as he puts it.[41] Stiglitz's main criticism is that the IMF and the World Bank have been taken over by market fundamentalist ideologues, with the result that policies have been forced on debtor countries by these institutions that have seriously damaged their social fabric. In applying the same doctrine everywhere, the IMF and the World Bank, he contends, were failing to take local conditions into account, and that often meant dismantling a public sector that was one of the largest employers in the country that was receiving their aid, as well as banishing subsidies that enabled the poorer sections of the population to afford basic goods and facilities. In most cases unemployment levels rose sharply once IMF/World Bank demands were put into practice, as did food prices, creating widespread public unrest as poverty became ever more acute. For Stiglitz, this was a travesty of what globalisation should have been achieving, and he remains convinced that a reformed version would increase living standards worldwide if it would only give up its market fundamentalist orientation with its insistence on cuts. Stiglitz himself, on the other hand, favours national economies striving to get 'as close to full employment as possible', by whatever means are needed.[42] While he is right that there is no necessary connection between globalisation and market fundamentalism, neoliberalism has such a strong grip on both the Western political class and the corporate sector that it is hard to see how the two can be disentangled in the present climate.

John Gray has been a consistent critic of market fundamentalism for some time now, and regards it as based on a series of 'delusions', primarily the one that believes free market capitalism represents the ideal economic system at all times and in all places: the 'one-size-fits-all' approach would appear to be encoded in neoliberalism's DNA. Unbridled laissez-faire capitalism is, he argues instead, a historical accident that came about because of a particular set of conditions which were unique to nineteenth-century Britain when industrialisation took off in earnest. He regards it as folly to go on as if those conditions still apply, or could be re-created, in what has since become a far more complex world geopolitically. There is, in other words, nothing inevitable about the spread of neoliberalism. Gray paints a gloomy picture of the world under neoliberalism as one where elites grow richer and the majority of the world's population is left in a state of economic insecurity, but on a more positive note he thinks that the system has too many internal contradictions for it to last indefinitely, prophesying that '[l]ike other twentieth-century utopias' it 'will be swallowed into the memory hole of history'.[43] Unfortunately, the message that seems to be communicated by the credit crisis is that we are all too able to consign the contradictions of the system to the memory-hole, rather than the system itself: that is how the fetish works.

Naomi Klein is even more critical of the globalisation ethic than Stiglitz is, and very much in favour of direct action programmes against the multinationals which most profit from it, as her book *No Logo* makes clear:

> [A]s connections have formed across national lines, a different agenda has taken hold, one that embraces globalization but seeks to wrest it from the grasp of the multinationals. Ethical shareholders, culture jammers, street reclaimers, McUnion organizers, human-rights hacktivists, school-logo fighters and Internet corporate watchdogs are at the early stages of demanding a citizen-centred alternative to the international rule of the brands.[44]

Klein identifies a growing surge of anger against the multinationals, but eleven years after she published the book they are nevertheless still major forces in society, and have if anything grown stronger through the boom years of neoliberalism which ended so abruptly with the credit crisis: as David Harvey has pointed out, one of the unintended consequences of neoliberal policies has been to help expedite the growth of monopolies. Anti-corporate activism has its role to play in any anti-profit movement, but its failure to date to change the commercial landscape is further proof of just how deep neoliberalism has dug into the Western psyche. The multinationals are only doing what the system both allows and encourages them to do, maximising profits for their shareholders, and as consumers we are still all too easily seduced by the lure of goods produced by cheap labour in sweatshop conditions in the developing world. It is a lure that becomes all the harder to resist in tough economic times when budgets become ever tighter, as the corporate sector is only too aware. Klein outlines these conditions in admirable detail, but sad to say, once again the fetish enables us both to take and not take these in, simultaneously.[45]

Maximising profits by keeping wage costs as low as possible also applies in the West, and companies can be quite ingenious as to how to achieve this goal. The phenomenon of internship might be reflected on in this respect, and many companies now factor this into their workplans as a wage-saving exercise as much as anything. It was originally a mainly American activity but it has become increasingly popular in European countries like the UK in recent years, to the extent of becoming something of a political issue about the dubious ethics of the system. It is still a recognised part of the 'old-boy network' with those in positions of power and influence using it as a way of getting their children's careers under way, but companies are now raiding the graduate market in a much more methodical way that builds up what is in effect an unpaid workforce. There is now a captive clientele for what has become a very wide-spread practice, exacerbated by rising graduate unemployment in a poor economic climate; as a recent book on the topic pointed out, 'pressure to do an internship is now simply part of being young', and it is to be found in 'virtually every industry and almost every country'.[46] It is unlikely to be a philanthropic impulse that is driving this phenomenon either, although companies do tend to claim just that: 'valuable work experience for the young', 'something to put on your CV', etc. The bottom line is that the more interns you take in then the more you save on junior staff wages, and companies are catching on to this fast and exploiting it for all it is worth. The more you save on wages, of course, then the more there is to share around on shareholder dividends and senior management bonuses, and that is the dream scenario for neoliberals.

A school of de-growth economists has emerged in recent years, and it is instructive to consider what they are propounding and why. Serge Latouche's work is particularly influential in this area of enquiry. In *Farewell to Growth*, Latouche is committed to what he rather jauntily calls 'convivial contraction' in the economic sphere, a process which exhorts us to 're-evaluate, reconceptualize, restructure, redistribute, relocalize, reduce, re-use and recycle'.[47] Yet Latouche is anything but jaunty when he sums up the reasons why he feels we need to opt for convivial contraction: 'Where are we going? We are heading for a crash. We are in a performance car that has no driver, no reverse gear and no brakes and it is going to slam into the limitations of the planet.'[48] Despite the weight of evidence for such an assessment coming through from a variety of sources, however, 'we refuse to listen because we know where our next meal is coming from', which very neatly captures the working of the fetish.[49] The only answer for Latouche is to sign up for a policy of de-growth, and he really is emphasising the 'de-' part of the equation, arguing that in the case of his own country, France, it would call for a reduction in national production and consumption by about two-thirds to stay within the limitations of the planet.

Latouche is careful to point out that de-growth is not to be considered the same as negative growth, which differentiates him from the more radical wing of the Green movement, nor equivalent to sustainable development, which differentiates him from the rest of the Greens. Rather, de-growth is to be thought of as akin to atheism in relation to religion; that is, a rejection of a particular faith, the 'gospel of growth for the sake of growth'.[50] Latouche feels we have to transcend the bankrupt ideology of modernity, with its relentless creation of more 'needs'. For Latouche it is a question of separating out our primary needs from our secondary; we may need shoes, but do we really need ten pairs as opposed to just one or two? A range of practical policies designed to lead us to the desired condition of de-growth is put forward, Latouche aiming himself firmly at politi-

cal activists searching for ways to effect change in our production-
and profit-obsessed culture, where, in the words of the French
author Dominique Belpomme, '[g]rowth has become humanity's
cancer.'[51]

Convivial contraction means emphasising social life over con-
sumerism; redefining what we really mean by concepts like wealth
and poverty; restructuring our society so that it no longer serves
the dictates of capitalism, but instead the changed social values
associated with de-growth; redistributing wealth from the rich and
powerful 'North' to the poor and economically exploited 'South';
moving to a localised system of production wherever this is possible; reducing overall consumption of goods and services (a stric-
ture Latouche also applies to mass tourism, which he dismisses as
an environmental disaster); recycling far more intensively than we
now do, encouraging manufacturers to produce products that break
down into component parts which invite re-use in a variety of con-
texts. Latouche concedes his is a utopian project, but feels it can be
achieved none the less, otherwise there would be no point at all in
politics, which should always hold out the prospect of change with
regard to ideological paradigms: 'If we want it, we can have another
world that is at once desirable, necessary and possible.'[52] That world
will be firmly focused on the local, which Latouche thinks holds the
key to reviving interest in participation in politics, giving us all as
citizens a stake in how our society develops: a Big Society model
perhaps, but one without the commitment to economic growth. It
all adds up to a plea to care more for each other's welfare, not just
locally but internationally, to be more socially responsible and to
jettison the self-interested individualism of neoliberalism.

De-growth's ultimate goal would appear to be local self-
sufficiency based on the materials available in any given geographical context. Other commentators see cutting back on what Latouche
provocatively calls 'hypergrowth' as an unacceptable solution to
our current ills.[53] Diane Coyle, for example, argues strongly against
what she calls the 'economics of enough', and sets out to defend
not just growth, but our expectations of growth, and, despite its
periodic failures, the market system designed to bring about that

growth: 'We tend to think of "growth" in an abstract way, but what it means in practice is access to an ever-increasing array of goods and services, and ever-greater command for each individual over how they want to lead their life.'[54] She goes on to claim that having this command leads to an 'increase in consumers' well-being', and thinks any attempt to rein this back would only ever appeal to a few.[55] If you want ten pairs of shoes rather than one or two, then that should be your right.

Essentially, what Coyle believes has gone wrong is that we have failed to adapt our institutions to meet the changes wrought by the new technology: improve these and move towards properly sustainable development, and the problems the economic crisis has posed us will largely disappear. There is nothing wrong with the current system that a few structural changes cannot solve, and concepts like de-growth are dismissed as misguided, possibly even anti-democratic in the way they seek to lessen the amount of control that we have over our lives as individuals in a thriving economy. Advocates of de-growth, however, would see 'command' as a trait implanted in us by neoliberalism, something of a fifth column since it induces us to act in precisely the way that the free market wants: that is, to buy, buy, and buy again, and never be satisfied with our present store of possessions but always on the lookout for the new and different. The market is only too happy to provide us with ten pairs of shoes, and will do its best to convince us that we really need an eleventh, twelfth, thirteenth, and so on into the indefinite future. All of which, as far as the de-growth school of thought goes, merely takes us that much further down the road to the inevitable crash of the planet's ecosystem. Command is, ultimately, an illusion from this perspective; but as long as it sustains the fetish then neoliberals will keep giving us the same message.

Home is Where the Profit Is

A particularly telling example of how the profit motive has infiltrated our daily lives can be found in the attitude to home ownership that has developed over the course of the economic good times leading up to the credit crisis. This can only be described in terms of an addiction. We were invited by both banks and politicians to regard our homes not as essentially places to live but as sources of profit, as investments, and with house prices rising year by year, often quite steeply, that seemed to be an entirely reasonable attitude to adopt. Property was to be considered as latent profit, and the bigger your mortgage then the brighter your future prospects promised to be – and the more the banks were willing to lend you on the basis of your assumed future collateral. Eventually, such loans were being extended with something like reckless abandon: hence the rise of the sub-prime mortgage market in the USA, which created a whole new class of mortgage holders who previously would have been considered far too high-risk to take a chance on. As events have subsequently proved, the original assessment was all too correct, leaving mortgage lenders with a string of defaulted loans and a sizeable collection of unsellable properties on their hands; but in the zeitgeist of the times back in the early 2000s risk exercised an irresistible appeal on the financial industry, and as long as the market was booming there seemed no reason to cut back on it.

The debt mountain that resulted from such practices was considered proof of economic prosperity, and we were enthusiastically exhorted to keep it growing, transforming us in no time into what some commentators have dubbed 'the debt generation'.[56] We all know where this merry-go-round ended: in a global financial crash, and in the eventual bankruptcy not just of individuals and companies but whole countries. Ireland quite literally bet its future on the property market, with the banks enthusiastically leading the way, and when this market nosedived in the aftermath of the crisis then so did the Irish economy, which proceeded to require several massive bailouts by its European Union partners to prevent it from collapsing altogether. The national debt there stood at a staggering €98.4 billion in December 2010, and it will need a massive upturn in the global economy, of which there is precious little sign at present, before the country can begin to achieve anything like economic stability again – never mind regain its once proud status as the 'Celtic tiger'. As happened in Iceland when its banks foundered immediately after the crisis hit, emigration is rapidly rising, indicating that Ireland's citizens have little confidence in the prospects for their economy.

House prices have fallen sharply across the West in the last few years, and banks have become notoriously reluctant to grant mortgages: the exact antithesis of what was happening immediately before the crash. So in neoliberal terms we have all got much poorer on that front, disappointed to discover that our property investment really could go down as well as up. But in real terms, we were living in a fetish world here again. The profit locked up in our house could only be realised if we sold it, and since we still had to live somewhere, which would require us to invest any profit made in another property, then that profit was always somewhat notional. There were exceptions of course: you might be engaged in downsizing, or selling an inherited property, or be a speculator in the housing market with several properties to your name. For the vast majority of us, however, a house was still in the first instance a place to live rather than an investment as such, and short of selling it and moving into a caravan, we stood unlikely ever to see much of its profit quotient. We knew this, somewhere in our mind, but at the same time we allowed ourselves to be seduced into thinking that just by living someplace and slowly paying off our mortgage we were becoming steadily, in boom periods sometimes even dramatically, richer. We had become so addicted to the neoliberal outlook, to the notion that turning a profit was the main point of our lives, that we refused to acknowledge its contradictions. Yet when commentators are looking around for signs of an economic upturn, one of the first things that they latch on to as a positive indicator is any improvement in property prices: the addiction persists.

Western banks may have become much more cautious about granting property loans since the crash, but the same has not applied in China, widely touted as the world's next economic superpower and a country that has been engaged in a massive construction programme for some time now, stoking up its property market. Fears are beginning to be expressed in the West as to whether the Chinese financial industry might have overextended itself in the mortgage market, with both the high-profile credit agency Fitch and *The Financial Times* raising this issue of late. It could well be, as a recent commentator has put it, that a new property bubble might be on the way, and as recovery from the last one is proving so difficult to engineer, that is not a pleasant prospect to contemplate.[57]

7
Global Warming and Profit

If anything summed up the degree of fetishisation that our society has succumbed to, it would have to be David Cameron's appeal to join in the fight against global warming because it would be a new source of profit, especially to those who got in on the ground floor before there was much competition. The idea that there had to be this kind of a sweetener in it to make the commercial world interested in addressing global warming, when their activities – and the massive profits they had been gaining from them throughout modern times – had been largely responsible for creating the environmental problem in the first place, is more than somewhat shocking. But I suspect it is an argument we shall be hearing more and more frequently over the course of the next few years, in line with the Friedman doctrine that a corporation's primary obligation is to seek profit for its owners and shareholders.

One would have thought that saving the planet took precedence over exploiting it, no matter what the cost might turn out to be: we've no place else to go, after all. The lure of immediate profit over the safety of future generations is so far proving to be the stronger force, however, and most of the time governments go along with this. It is highly ironic that 'conservative' politicians worldwide generally show so little interest in, or commitment to, 'conservation' as such. The oil companies, as a notorious case in point, are mostly in a state of outright denial over global warming, refusing to accept that they are even implicated in it in any meaningful way. On the contrary, they keep seeking out new sources of oil, no matter how inaccessible their geographical location or how disruptive they threaten to be to the surrounding environment: the recently exploited Athabasca tar sands in northern Canada stand as a stark warning on that latter score, given the large-scale despoliation of a significant tract of wilderness that it has entailed. Unless we can move away from the profit motive then this state of affairs is likely to continue, so it becomes ever more important to make the case for an anti-profit movement: to prioritise saving, and sharing publicly, over exploiting.

Warming, the Modern, and the Postmodern

Global warming is the product of a modern age characterised by its restless search for technological progress, very much in the service of the profit motive: 'a symptom of a particular development path', as a *Nature* article put it.[1] Yet for all the criticism of modernity and its goals by postmodernists, technological progress remains just as much an obsession now as it ever was for the moderns. Each new step forward in technology – cars, computers, mobile phones and the entire range of electronic goods, etc. – equals a massive new source of profit for those who have invested in it, and if it does succeed in improving the lifestyle of us all eventually, it is noticeable that the benefits are very unequally spread. The general public will always lag behind the gains made by the entrepreneurial class in this respect, and the public in the developing world far more so than their counterparts in the developed. From the Industrial Revolution onwards this has been the clear pattern, a point that social commentators have been making as forcefully as they could from the days of Thomas Carlyle and Karl Marx onwards: as Carlyle so pointedly described it, the 'cash nexus' had taken over when it came to human relationships and how we viewed the world.[2]

What has also been a clear pattern since the Industrial Revolution is that the greater the technological progress that is made, then the greater the increase in global population. That increase creates a need for more goods which in its turn increases production, therefore carbon emissions, across the globe as well. The increase in population has been dramatic, a case of doubling in the last fifty years alone and with no apparent end in sight at present. Even if the living standards in most of the developing world, where the greatest increases in population have been taking place in our time, are very poor then it still all adds up to a significantly larger amount of carbon being released into the planet's atmosphere. Carbon levels there are already felt by scientists to be dangerously high, but unless some systematic programme of reduction is begun almost immediately then the levels can only continue to rise. Yet each rise in those levels equals extra profit for someone, and to bring them down requires a massive investment that so far is not forthcoming from either the public or the private sector. In textbook Friedmanite fashion, shareholders do not as a rule take kindly to the idea of diverting company profits into schemes in the public realm, no matter how humanitarian the purpose may be, and governments in a neoliberal age are generally very reluctant to raise taxes for any purpose at all. The demonisation of government taxation is one of the defining features of neoliberalism as an ideology, and even previously staunchly social democratic polities have been persuaded to institute tax-cutting regimes to free up capital for greater entrepreneurial activity.

The private sector's interest in reduction of the carbon levels is only likely to be gained if it can see that there is a new source of profit awaiting it there; and in keeping with the sector's ethos and responsibilities towards its shareholders, it will have to be a source of profit that requires as little investment on its part as possible and that yields a fairly quick return. Green technology is long-term, and the market for it is as yet unpredictable; standard, carbon-emitting technology is short-term and reliably profitable right now. Unless the process is started by public money one suspects that development in the area of green technology will not get very far, since the private sector is rarely, if ever, motivated by any notion of the public welfare. In that sense, David Cameron is correct to stress the profit motive to try to generate interest from that sector, but it remains an indictment of our short-sightedness that he has felt the need to do so. Securing our environmental future cannot be reduced to a debate about relative profit margins; the priorities just seem all wrong, but that is what 'no-rules' capitalism has succeeded in imposing on us.

Denialism and the Age of Conspiracy

There is, however, a very vocal lobby of 'denialists' questioning the fact of global warming, or casting doubt on the projections being made on how such warming will affect the environment in years to come. The oil companies have proved only too keen to support this lobby with funding to do their research, and have done their best to sow seeds of doubt in the public mind over the substantial body of scientific findings, accepted by the vast majority of those in that community, which claim that it is already well under way in terms of its adverse effect on the Earth's ecosystems.[3] It has to be admitted that such doubt is quite widespread amongst a public that is genuinely confused as to who to believe – and the more apocalyptic scenarios of such as James Lovelock, with their visions of a planet almost devoid of human life a few generations hence, do not necessarily help matters on this front either.[4] Quite possibly, all that such prophecies do is to induce a sense of fatalism in us. It is all too easy to become desensitised by the more sensationalist claims being made by such theorists – Lovelock is not alone in making them, although he does tend to be the most melodramatic[5] – and to turn instead to the more comforting statements of the denialists who promise that everything will be fine, and that even if the problem does exist it is perfectly manageable anyway, merely a matter of tinkering a bit with the environment here and there when specific problems happen to arise.[6] This is the kind of terrain on which the fetish comes into its own. And the media are only too happy to provide a platform for the denialists to make their case, as the controversy so aroused generates public interest that boosts their audience share.

The 'Climategate' episode of 2009, in which climate scientists at the University of East Anglia were accused of blocking the publication of papers that disagreed with their belief in global warming, undoubtedly badly damaged the scientific community, making the public even more receptive to denialist readings of the situation. These claims proceeded to come thick and fast in the media, which positively revelled in bringing to light such apparent scientific duplicity in what was claimed to amount to a giant scam perpetrated by a self-serving scientific community. The episode merely seemed to confirm various sceptical accounts that had already been circulating widely in the media questioning the validity of the scientific evidence for warming, such as Channel 4's 'The Great Global Warming Swindle' in 2007. The programme generated a storm of controversy, leading to Channel 4 being investigated by the UK's broadcasting regulator Ofcom, which came to the decision that while there was misrepresentation of some scientists' views in the programme, there was nevertheless no deliberate attempt to mislead the public, merely a desire to present alternative views that challenged mainstream orthodoxies. Other commentators were less kind, accusing the channel of sensationalism and a cavalier disregard for scientific fact. As *The Observer*'s science correspondent, Robin McKie, wearily remarked, '[w]e live in an age of conspiracies', and Channel 4 was pandering to what had become an 'internet-fuelled' craze, adding nothing of note to the debate by its one-sided intervention.[7] The effect of Climategate, however, was to fuel this craze even further, with the popular press only too happy to stoke up the controversy.

That the scientists involved in Climategate were eventually exonerated from any conspiratorial wrongdoings predictably enough attracted far fewer headlines from the same quarter, except amongst the more heavyweight titles in the national press, and in fact is possibly still not all that well known to the public at large. Polls regularly tend to show that public opinion is still very much divided on the issue of whether global warming is a reality or just a confidence trick on the part of some self-interested scientists eager to keep research grants flowing into their institutions. The oil companies are only too willing to encourage such a belief as the latter, and to play down the need for green technology, or at least any large-scale application of it. Since the cost of any wholesale switchover to green power will have to be borne by governments, which is to say the general public and the tax base it provides, there is a reluctance to move away from the tried and true, especially since it seems to be so reliable in its delivery. It is reliable in terms of its profit margins too, so we can expect a general conservatism amongst those involved in it in the private sector, even if we have to note that the reliability unfortunately enough extends to its highly damaging effect on the earth's biosphere.

The Protocol of Subtle Denialism

The reluctance to move away from fossil fuels, the very life-blood of modernity as we have understood it with its constant demand for energy to drive production, can be seen most strikingly in the international response to the many warnings coming out of the scientific community about how much of a threat global warming poses to the world. The UN-sponsored International Panel on Climate Change (IPCC) puts out regular reports with increasingly dire predictions about where global warming could lead us. All too often these are met with either apathy or hostility from the political classes internationally in what might be construed as a more subtle form of denialism, even though many scientists have criticised the IPCC for being overly cautious in their projections. We are told that melting icecaps could cause sea levels to rise to such an extent that the world's coastal areas, where a large proportion of the world's largest and most important cities are located, would be wiped out; that deserts could expand dramatically in size, laying waste vast tracts of agricultural land; that rainfall patterns could change drastically, with drought spreading over huge areas that are currently heavily populated; that agricultural patterns would be severely affected thus problematising global food provision; that tropical diseases would gradually make their way north putting increasing numbers of the world's population at risk from conditions such as malaria. Some of these problems are already beginning to manifest themselves: low-lying islands are gradually being swamped (the Tuvalu islanders in the Pacific have already drawn up plans for evacuation to New Zealand, and Kiribati has been in similar negotiations); drought is a serious factor in large parts of Africa and Australia; rainfall patterns do seem to be getting much more erratic than in the recent past; the insects that carry tropical diseases are being noticed in much higher latitudes than has been their norm.

Yet even when governments agree to address the overall problem of warming and set some targets, as they did in the Kyoto Protocol of 1997, the results are generally very disappointing. When it involves any great sacrifice nationally, governments are all too prone to opt out or to fudge the issue such that nothing very much actually gets done. Targets are shifted or amended downwards, inconclusive talks are held, and subtle denialism comes into play. The USA, for example, refused to follow any of the Kyoto recommendations on the grounds that to do so would harm the national economy. Needless to say, without any support from that quarter – the world's largest source of carbon emissions at the point the Protocol was agreed, although China is fast catching up and on course to surpass the US – little of real substance has been achieved in response to the targets set for each nation. What is in reality a global concern requiring transnational cooperation has instead been reduced to a national issue centring on each nation's economy and how its relative global competitiveness would be affected by compliance with the Protocol. So far there is precious little sign that anyone is willing to accord compliance greater priority than their GDP. There is a desperate need for a global social brain to come into operation on this issue, but so far that is being blocked by a neoliberal mindset, which can only think of economic growth, *homo economicus*, the free market, and profit.

Green for Profit?

What is the potential for significant profit in green technology, and could that be enough to stem the onward march of global warming? The first thing to be said is that the viability of most of the techniques to generate green energy are still very much open to question. Solar power, wind power, and wave power all have their advocates and are already in operation at various points around the globe; but they also have their drawbacks and it is unclear whether they could ever produce energy on the scale, and with the degree of reliability, that fossil fuel systems so consistently do, or at a comparable cost. So the profit side of the equation is unclear too. Unless such systems become mass producers then they will remain niche markets, and niche markets are not where the really big profits are made, meaning that the multinationals will not feel any strong sense of motivation to invest heavily there. Admittedly there has been some attention paid to these areas by the multinationals, but little indication that any of them feel this is anything much more than just a sideline – undertaken, perhaps, to improve their public image as much as anything else: 'look how much we care about the environment', etc. – or that they have a responsibility to the public to become more deeply involved. Again, the public interest will never be a primary concern of business; not unless ignoring it is impacting adversely on profit margins, which is about the only thing that would ever affect the Friedman protocol. We cannot expect to experience much in the way of corporate altruism.

Some areas of green technology are fairly well developed, however, with solar power already being used to generate significant amounts of electricity in various parts of the globe and attracting a certain amount of corporate attention. Germany, surprisingly enough given its less than ideal climate, has become a very significant player in this market. American companies have taken advantage of the country's hot desert climates in the South-Western states to set up some large-scale installations of solar panels, and these have been successful enough to inspire expansion in this area. The companies involved, such as Abengoa Solar, sound bullish about the future too:

Abengoa Solar has signed an agreement with Arizona Public Service (APS), the largest electric company in Arizona, to build and operate what will be the largest solar power plant in the world. Recently, the White House announced [July 2010] that DOE Department of Energy has offered a conditional commitment for a $1.45 billion loan guarantee to Abengoa Solar, Inc. The loan will support the construction and start-up of Solana. The plant will be installed about 70 miles southwest of Phoenix, near Gila Bend. Solana, with 250 MW nets of power output capacity, is based on parabolic trough technology and thermal storage using molten salts. When operation starts up, the plant will have the capacity to supply clean power to 70,000 homes and will eliminate around 475,000 tons of CO_2.[8]

The company speaks of the plant as creating, either directly or indirectly, several thousand jobs, and clearly considers itself to be the market leader in paving the way to a more sustainable energy future for the USA.

Areas like the Sahara are also being eyed up for future development, and it has even been suggested that the Middle East could switch from being the leading source of fossil fuels to the leading one of solar power, given that it has the ideal terrain for this in thousands of square miles of hot, arid deserts:

> In a recent interview, European energy commissioner Günther Oettinger said that Europe will be importing hundreds of megawatts of solar-generated electricity from north Africa within five years. The EU is committed to sourcing 20% of its energy from renewable sources by 2020. Most advanced in the planning is the German-led Desertec Industrial Initiative, which aims to provide 15% of Europe's electricity by 2050 or earlier, via power lines stretching across the desert and the Mediterranean. Its $400bn plan is supported by some of Germany's biggest companies, including Siemens, E.On and Deutsche Bank.[9]

Investment is beginning to build up in this area of renewable energy, therefore, but whether all such plans collectively will be enough, or come in time, to halt global warming is another question.

Cost is still a factor in solar power, although increased investment is beginning to bring it down, to the point that it may well soon be able to compete with more conventionally produced power. But again, we are relying on the market to be the determinant as to whether this method of energy supply takes off on the large scale or not, rather than the far more pressing issue of environmental impact, and we cannot rely on the market to put the public before profit.

Profit could undoubtedly be made if any of the more extreme projects being mooted for geoengineering were ever given the go-ahead, unlikely though that is at present, especially given the potentially enormous cost involved in setting most of them up. Geoengineers tend to think on the very grandest of scales and their projected schemes generally require cutting-edge technology that can be very expensive to implement. They are also unpredictable in how they might affect the Earth system: still an issue of some debate in science circles, where it is argued that our understanding of the complex interaction of the many parts of the Earth system still has significant gaps. The practicalities of putting any of these into operation can be quite mind-boggling to contemplate. Shooting huge numbers of mirrors into space to reflect sunlight back on itself and thus away from the Earth, 16 trillion in one of the more daring projects put forward using this principle of 'sunshading', will not come cheap. There would be an estimated cost of $5 trillion in the example just given, although the companies involved, and of course their shareholders, would do very well out of such an exercise.[10] Under the current economic paradigm it is hard to see such schemes being removed from the market altogether, in the sense that governments will be purchasing the necessary equipment – 16 trillion mirrors, etc. – from the private sector. Other schemes are no less grandiose, if easier to envisage, such as the suggestion that we cover vast tracts of the world's deserts in white sheeting in order to reflect sunlight back into space ('albedo enhancement', as it is called[11]), and possibly also consider painting our houses white to achieve the same effect.

Geoengineering will remain just so many pipe-dreams and blueprints without huge investment, however, and investment on a scale that will deter the private sector from developing it on its own. For the time being, profit can be more easily accumulated elsewhere.

Arguably the easiest and most reliable method of making profit out of green technology is through biofuels, which require no feats of geoengineering in their production, simply land for cultivation of the plants used in the process. The process is well-developed and the technology straightforward, and biofuel is already in use in many countries around the world. Great claims have been made for biofuels as the future for cars, on the grounds that they involve far fewer carbon emissions from their engines than petrol does, and such vehicles are already on the market. But the downsides are becoming increasingly apparent, and those claims are beginning to be contested. For a start, in order to be produced on a commercial scale biofuels require vast tracts of land on which to grow the plants needed. British companies alone have bought up 3.2 million hectares throughout Africa for this purpose. Producers claim this is generally land which is not fit for agriculture, although this seems to be open to question and many critics are beginning to raise objections, arguing that the effect of biofuel cultivation is to push food prices up globally. Oxfam has even claimed that the cost of staple foods will probably at least double within the next twenty years. It is the world's poorest nations that are hit hardest by this phenomenon, and as Oxfam's chief executive has put it, '[w]e are sleepwalking towards an age of avoidable crisis' on this front.[12]

Biofuels may not be as carbon-friendly as they appear either, in that forest land is often cleared to make way for biofuel crops, such as in the Amazon basin, and forests are a major source of carbon absorption; so depleting them significantly around the globe has an adverse effect as far as global warming goes. Unfortunately enough, given the soaring price of oil in recent years, the demand for biofuel is only too likely to go up, so the projections on food price increases may well have to be revised upwards too.

Carbon is Profit

If there is still doubt as to how much scope for profit there really is in the green energy market, there is none at all when it comes to the carbon version that has been our staple for so long. Oil remains big business, yielding correspondingly big profits, and despite all the threats that we are either reaching or have in fact passed 'peak oil', the point at which global stocks will continue to dwindle for this unrenewable resource, the oil companies seem adept at finding enough new sources of their product to keep them going into the immediate future. Perhaps the fetish is doing its work here again. We're aware that peak oil signals that the resource in question is finite, but each discovery of a new pocket of it, in no matter how currently inaccessible a location – beneath the Arctic Ocean and icecap, as a case in point – is enough to keep us from addressing the problem. Mountain ranges also can be a source of oil through shale, which can be ground up to release the oil contained in the rocks, so we might expect that to be turned to next in desperation once we exhaust the newly discovered undersea fields. What any such concerted effort in that direction will do to the world's landscape will be a secondary consideration as far as the oil companies are concerned, and, although shale extraction can be more expensive than standard methods, mountain ranges pose far fewer logistical problems in terms of accessibility than deep-sea drilling in remote and inhospitable areas of the world. The technique is already extensively used in China.

And we have to realise that oil really does mean substantial profit, as can be seen from this BBC report on Shell Oil:

> The oil giant Shell has reported profits almost doubled from $9.8bn to $18.6bn (£11.5bn) for 2010, partly thanks to rising oil prices and output. Its chief executive, Peter Voser, said the company had made good progress and that there was 'still more to come'.[13]

Still more profits to come means still more global warming to come as well, but with profits available on this scale one can see why it is that the oil industry chooses to encourage scepticism about the latter phenomenon, and also why its shareholders would be only too happy to go along with this. Climategates are a gift to this constituency, and we can be sure they will be quick to exploit anything of a similar nature that crops up in future.

Conclusion

Global warming is largely the result of our obsession with profit, therefore, and it is deeply ironic that we now seem to be relying on that same obsession to be the answer to the problem. It is as if we are always treating symptoms not causes, assuming that the profit motive will be our saviour rather than, as past experience suggests is far more likely to be the case, merely presenting us with yet another set of problems. That is increasingly how things stand in healthcare too, as the next chapter will show.

8
Healthcare and Profit

Healthcare is an area where there are vast profits to be made, particularly for those in the drug industry: 'Big Pharma' in popular parlance. It is also an area where the ethical problems generated by the profit motive most dramatically come to a head. Making profit out of human sickness, pain, and misery would seem to verge on the despicable; but as long as healthcare is either in private hands, or widely exposed to the demands of the private sector, then it will, unfortunately enough, continue to be an attractive prospect to commercial entrepreneurs. I do not include trained healthcare professionals in this group; they must be remunerated properly for their efforts on our behalf according to their skills and experience, particularly given the very substantial, one is tempted to say unethical, fees involved in studying for a medical degree these days.[1] The point of the creation of publicly funded health services – such as the UK's National Health Service, and its various equivalents throughout Western Europe – was to minimise the profit motive in this area, with the goal of making healthcare available to all and not just to the wealthy and well-connected, which was the general pattern pre-mid-twentieth century. The NHS, however, has been forced by a succession of governments in recent decades to introduce elements of privatisation into its daily operations wherever possible, and the cuts to the public sector in the wake of the credit crisis are speeding up this process quite considerably. Since the NHS eats up a considerable amount of government annual spending (£119.5 billion in 2010, or 18 per cent), this is a policy we can expect to be continued.

The current coalition government has opted for a radical overhaul of the NHS, a move which invites ever greater private involvement in the provision of services across the board, from portering through to serious operations. Grave concerns are being expressed about this initiative by the British medical profession, with the BMA warning that it will most likely lead to a reduction in overall quality of care as well as to the creation of a much less egalitarian system than we have hitherto enjoyed. This would represent something of a return to the 1930s, with those at the bottom end of the socio-economic scale losing out, as some prominent members of the profession have been warning is only too likely to occur if the reforms go through as planned.[2] The fact that this is being done in the name of setting the NHS 'free' (to make profits out of its activities, for one thing; such as taking on more private, fee-paying, patients), is an indication of just how determined a campaign is being waged by advocates of privatisation against the very concept of public service. All this despite the fact that in a recent large-scale survey of doctors in eleven countries conducted by the Commonwealth Fund, the NHS was rated as arguably the all-round most effective national medical service in the world.[3] This not the same thing as saying that it is perfect and in no need of improvement, but many of its imperfections are the result of underfunding rather than a lack of professionalism on the part of its staff.

It could well be that the government will pull back from some of the planned reorganisation plans given the amount of public opposition that has been stirred up by these; but it is in the nature of the neoliberal temperament never to let things rest when it comes to public services, and to keep coming back with new schemes after the fuss subsides. Bit by bit these serve to eat away at the concept of public service, and each time around at least some advance is made in shifting some of this towards the private sector. The neoliberal hope is that at some point it becomes just too difficult or too expensive to return to the old system, and the public just has to get used to this, even if in resigned fashion. Once largely privatised, it would require substantial tax increases to return the NHS to public control, and these are generally guaranteed to make any government lose popularity in the short term, threatening its chances in the next election. This is a situation that plays right into the hands of neoliberals, who can exploit our individual reluctance to see our earnings reduced. It is all too easy to believe, as a recent book on the topic has it, that there is a conspiratorial plot in operation against the NHS[4] – and it is very much impelled by the spirit of neoliberalism, the notion that all human activities must submit to the discipline of the market.

This chapter considers the impact of privatisation on the public at large, and by way of a case study compares the NHS with the American health system (largely funded by private health insurance schemes run for profit, with minimal government involvement), to show just how problematical it can be when profit becomes the dominant factor in such a critical area of human existence. None of us, after all, can escape needing medical attention at various points over the course of our lives: it is not an optional extra, it is simply part of being human to require such treatment. Yet at least some elements in British political life feel that profit is an essential component of any institutional activity, and are determined to put their beliefs into practice, no matter what opposition they may arouse. Thus the NHS is to be 'liberated' from politics in order to take its rightful place in the market.[5] It is the usual rationale that is being trotted out in justification: private means more efficient and cheaper, public means costly and wasteful. Little hard evidence is ever offered for such a strategy, it is taken as read, pretty much as an article of faith. Whether it will be as fair is never really examined, that is never a market consideration; some products and services may make the world a better place, but that will never be more than a by-product to their main purpose, which is to make as much profit as possible for entrepreneurs and shareholders. Yet the more frequently it is asserted as a gospel truth that private always trumps public when it comes to providing a service – accompanied by a few carefully calculated and strategic uses of emotive words like 'liberating', 'free', and 'freedom', not to mention 'reform' with its implication that something is wrong and needs to be corrected – then the more it promotes the development of the fetish. The rhetoric is carefully chosen, but what it is promising and what it will actually deliver are by no means the same thing.

One of the fears that arises over bringing outside competition into a service like the NHS is that the profit motive most likely will dispose private health organisations, which have to answer to their shareholders after all, to 'cherry pick' those procedures which will be low-risk and cost the least, thus yielding a reliable profit. This would leave the NHS with all the expensive care, making it appear much less 'cost-effective' per patient and playing right into the hands of advocates of the virtues of the private system. The statistics could be made to appear very damning on this score, and no doubt the right-wing press would have a field day with them. American healthcare insurance schemes already show themselves very reluctant to take on high-maintenance clients, so we could expect the same thing to happen in the UK once profit starts to dictate the agenda. The less treatment that the private sector actually provides then the higher its profit margin will be. Once again this is not fair, but then that is not what the market is about, especially under 'no-rules capitalism'.

The USA Versus the UK

Even if you are in a medical plan in the USA you will generally be required to pay some percentage, or initial amount, of any health-care bills that you run up, which can become very burdensome when any major procedures or operations are required; and American hospital, or dental, care is not cheap. The part-payment system also applies in some of the European countries, as well as in other parts of the Western world like Canada, with similar rules to be found in operation in Australia and New Zealand. But in none of these systems will it cost the patient as much overall as it does in the USA. The NHS, too, now requires a certain amount of input from patients – on prescriptions, for example, or for dental care – but these are generally quite small compared with their American equivalents. Such payments are also waived in many instances, as they are in the case of patients with chronic, long-term conditions and the retired when it comes to prescriptions. In the American system on the other hand, prescriptions can be a major expense for the elderly, resulting in the interesting phenomenon of many American senior citizens travelling to Mexico in recent years in order to stock up on supplies of their medication, which is generally sold much more cheaply there over the counter; although some concern has been expressed about the quality control of the products being purchased. For those living in the north of the country Canada is an option, with many drugs also being sold at a lower cost there, leading to similar cross-border trips being made by seniors. Federal law has even been changed of late to allow American citizens to order prescription drugs from overseas by mail order, an illegal action beforehand, and of course the Internet has made this practice very much easier.

Healthcare premiums can also rise as you age in America, often quite dramatically, since then you are more likely to be in need of medical attention, and especially of expensive medical attention for major illnesses and conditions. It must always be remembered that contributors to healthcare schemes in America are viewed primarily as potential sources of profit rather than individuals for whom there is an ethical responsibility to provide aid: a point made very strongly in Michael Moore's film *Sicko*.[6] Older patients are not really in those schemes' interest, unless they are rich and can afford steeply increased premiums. All such companies do their best to cut loss-making activities: as Sergei Latouche notes, the new heroes of the business world are 'the cost killers', those managers who can keep outgoings to a minimum and whom corporations like the medical insurance giants 'fight to recruit by offering them stock options and golden parachutes'.[7] Cost killing equals profit-creation, the real business of private medical care. If this is to become the future in the UK then most of the population are going to be in for a very rude shock after life under the NHS.

What advocates of the American system never refer to, however, is how exclusive it is. There is the scandal, for example, of there being an estimated fifty million Americans who are not covered by any form of private healthcare at all, and for whom sickness until recently, and the introduction of the bitterly contested Obama reforms, constituted a personal catastrophe that they were in no way prepared to meet. Raj Patel, no great fan of the American healthcare system either, has remarked that 'almost every culture finds distasteful the notion that poverty should exclude anyone from medical care';[8] but figures like this are proof of how effective the fetish can be in overriding those feelings. In this respect, pictures in the press, and television reports, of temporary field hospitals set up by charities in various areas of the country offering free medical attention to anyone who turned up, came as something of a shock to European audiences. The effect was to make America appear more like a Third World nation than the world's richest, especially given the large crowds of would-be patients that such enterprises invariably attract. A press report of one such event, held for eight days in the LA Forum by a group called Remote Area Medical, painted a sombre picture of life for those fifty million without coverage:

> They came in their thousands, queuing through the night to secure one of the coveted wristbands offering entry into a strange parallel universe where medical care is a free and basic right and not an expensive luxury. Some of these Americans had walked miles simply to have their blood pressure checked, some had slept in their cars in the hope of getting an eye-test or a mammogram, others had brought their children for immunisations that could end up saving their life.[9]

The idea that such an event could take place in any of Britain's major cities is, at present anyway, unthinkable. That it was needed in Los Angeles, one of America's largest and richest cities, has to be a damning indictment of the American system as currently constituted. As one of Remote Area Medical's volunteer doctors pointedly noted: 'Healthcare needs reform, obviously. There are so many people falling through the cracks, who don't get care. That's why so many are here.'[10] That there is any need at all, never mind what appears to be a mass 'market', for a group like Remote Area Medical speaks volumes for the failings of the American system. The mere fact that it precludes such things occurring in the UK would be enough on its own to justify the existence of the NHS. Remote Area Medical's website describes it as 'a non-profit, volunteer, airborne relief corps dedicated to serving mankind by providing free health care, dental care, eye care, veterinary services, and technical and educational assistance to people in remote areas of the United States and the world', and they are certainly to be commended for their social conscience;[11] although one has to wonder by what criteria Los Angeles could ever count as 'remote'. One also has to wonder what happens to their patients when the field hospital closes up and moves elsewhere: continuity of care is an impossible dream under such circumstances. Remote Area Medical could stand as a warning as to what the Big Society may well end up looking like.

No doubt the Friedman line on this would be that the individuals in question, far from 'falling through the cracks', had instead been exercising their 'freedom' not to use their money for health insurance; as he argued was the case with Americans who had no pension plans, something else he was categorically opposed to there being any compulsory scheme instituted for by governments. But this assumes the individuals in question had the money to do so in the first place, and it is also to wash our hands as to the fates of their dependents, who can in no way be held responsible for their parents' decisions. The notion of there being cracks in the system is bad enough to contemplate, but for children to be falling through them is surely unacceptable in any economically advanced nation. To allow such things to happen on the grounds that publicly funded healthcare is to be equated with socialism, as the right in America keeps so loudly insisting, is ideological fundamentalism of the worst kind. Freedom in this case seems to mean little more than neglect. On that connection of publicly funded healthcare with socialism, the US military personnel have the bulk of their healthcare costs covered by the government-run Tricare programme. Yet no one has ever suggested that this is turning them into socialists. The government is beginning to worry about how much the scheme is costing however.[12]

The Harvard academic, and Senior Health Care Advisor to

President Obama, David M. Cutler, offers an insight into the thinking that led to the Obama administration's health reforms in his article 'The American healthcare system'.[13] Cutler identifies the basic problem of American healthcare as follows: 'American healthcare professionals know how to keep us healthy, but often they can not give patients the care they need because the medical system gets in their way.'[14] The reason this is so is the high degree of fragmentation to be found in the American system, with its mixture of public and private coverage and different rules and regulations in each state of the union turning it into an obstacle course for patients and doctors alike: 'An American doctor has to be a genius to know the rules for treating or taking care of each patient without getting questioned by the insurance companies or others.'[15] His solution is for the system to be rationalised, by which he means 'figuring out how to save money while delivering better care to more people. Right now, many independent estimates say that we overspend by 50 percent on healthcare.'[16] Part of the reason for that overspend, of course, is that so many of those involved in the country's healthcare, such as the insurance companies and 'Big Pharma', require profit for providing their services, putting into perspective the repeated claims of advocates that America spends far more per head on medical care than countries like the UK do. Not all of that expenditure is staying within the healthcare system per se, or going towards patient care. As Cutler pointedly notes, there is a pressing need to 'give insurance companies incentives to focus more on taking care of the sick than on coming up with rationales to insure only the healthy', but one suspects that will be a long and arduous exercise in an industry based on the profit motive.[17] To his credit, Cutler rejects the more extreme views of the neoliberal camp which advocate even less government involvement in healthcare than at present, arguing instead that as individuals we are not very good at planning for the future and that people in general need help when dealing with severe illnesses: 'leaving them adrift is not the way to go'.[18]

The statistics on healthcare coverage in America quoted by Cutler (2005 figures) make damning reading. Even though the government contributes 44.7 per cent of the country's overall health spending, 15.8 per cent of the population are without any form of medical insurance. There are government-run programmes such as Medicare and Medicaid, but they are quite selective about who qualifies for coverage, as the Medicare.gov site outlines:

Medicaid is for low income:
Pregnant women
Children under the age of 19
People 65 and over
People who are blind
People who are disabled
People who need nursing home care
Application for Medicaid is at the State's Medicaid agency.

Medicare is for:
People 65 and over
People of any age who have kidney failure or long term kidney disease
People who are permanently disabled and cannot work
Medicare is applied for at the local Social Security office.[19]

This offers a lifeline to some of the most needy and vulnerable sections of the population, but the fifty million or so Americans who fall through the cracks in the healthcare system reveal the considerable limitations of government help. Medicaid is means-tested and the criteria for eligibility vary from state to state, which further confuses the issue. There is certainly a wide diversity of treatment regimes on view, but whether this is to the benefit of either patients or doctors is another question entirely.

Cutler's point about the difficulty of getting to grips with America's fragmented system strikes home when we look at one of the giants of the American health insurance industry, the Blue Cross Blue Shield Association (BCBS). This is a confederation of thirty-nine independent organisations across the country covering around one hundred million Americans, roughly one in three of the population. This is a franchise operation consisting of a mixture of non-profit and for-profit companies, and their operations and attitudes can vary quite widely. One particular branch, the for-profit BCBSNC in North Carolina, has been the subject of criticism in the past for its substantial rate rises even in years of high profits, as well as for being notably expert in the art of cost killing to avoid having to meet subscribers' treatment bills. BCBSNC also controversially campaigned against President Obama's health reforms, although BSBC nationally claims to support these: 'The Blue Cross and Blue Shield companies are committed to working with the Administration and all other parties to implement this new law.'[20] The largest organisation in the BCBS Association is the WellPoint programme, which covers thirty-three million in fourteen states. Wellpoint reported income of $1.416 billion on turnover of $4.358 billion in 2010, so there really is substantial profit to be made in this industry. The fact that cost killing is absolutely integral to its economic success ought to give pause for thought, but it is unlikely to deter shareholders: put healthcare on the stock market and it becomes just another investment.

Liberation or Abandonment?

It is ideological fundamentalism that lies behind the UK government's plans for the NHS too, as the 2010 White Paper 'Equity and excellence: liberating the NHS' makes abundantly clear. The rhetoric deployed is carefully calculated to sound impeccably democratic and geared to the improvement of services for all, with much talk of patient choice, ownership of services by patients and hospital staff, and autonomy – and who is going to argue against any of those things? It is only when those concepts are unpacked that the fundamentalist imperative behind 'liberation' becomes apparent. When the document asserts that 'money will follow the patient' in the name of 'patient choice', for example, that can turn out to mean that money will follow the patient out of the NHS into the private sector, and the latter will of course take its cut for providing the required service.[21] How that will help to improve the NHS's quality of care is hard to work out, especially since, as pointed out earlier, the private sector is likely to be drawn towards the most lucrative, quick turn-round, low-risk services, and to leave the most expensive, difficult, ones to the NHS. Strip away the jargon and 'liberation' from 'micromanagement' by politicians begins to sound more like being abandoned to the vagaries of the market. We can elect the politicians or turn them out of office if we are unhappy with their style of micromanagement, but we have no such power over the market or its constantly changing cast of self-interested players.

'Choice' lies right at the heart of the neoliberal creed, and it is always presented as one of the great selling points of the market system: communist systems invariably came in for criticism for failing to offer consumers choice and diversity of product and service. 'Equity and excellence' equally sees the concept as central to its reforming plans. Much of what is said on choice in the document is unexceptionable – having the choice to consult your medical records, decide which course of treatment you would prefer after being told the options, etc. – but the crunch comes with promises such as 'all patients will have choice and control over their care and treatment, and choice of any willing provider wherever relevant'.[22] 'Any willing provider' assumes competition for NHS services, in other words the encroachment of the private sector, which in real terms means siphoning off resource from the NHS. Under the guise of choice, a mechanism for the creation of profit out of healthcare is being stealthily implemented. This is made explicit at a later point in the document when discussing the delegation of powers to GP consortia, a policy which is particularly opposed by the BMA:

> GP consortia will have the freedom to decide what commissioning activities they undertake for themselves and for what activities (such as demographic analysis, contract negotiation, performance monitoring and aspects of financial management) they may choose to buy in support from external organisations, including local authorities, private and voluntary sector bodies.[23]

Although GPs in general have shown very little enthusiasm for this policy, that has not deterred the government from pushing on with its plans in this area. One might also point out that the patient can only choose a provider if the consortium holding the budget is willing to meet the cost. If it is not willing, then one assumes the patient will either have to opt for something cheaper or meet the difference out of his or her own pocket: at which point we no longer have an egalitarian system.

The whole thrust of the White Paper is to move the NHS as far away as possible from direct political control, as if that would resolve almost all of its problems at a stroke. The assumption is that political control can only mean bureaucracy, and bureaucracy is one of neoliberalism's pet hates: it is bureaucracy that prevents the market from realising its full potential, and thus, from the neoliberal standpoint, having the opportunity to increase and guarantee our personal freedom. Government becomes little better than a benign monitor in such cases, ensuring that the market is given the conditions it wishes, because the market is being seen as the cure for pretty well all of our social ills. The ultimate logic of such an approach is that we hardly need any government at all, that the market can take over the vast majority of what we have traditionally regarded as government's core concerns, with the latter turning into the market's cheerleader. It is full-blown Friedmanism, and its faith in the market seems absolute. Indeed, the first of the economic regulating body Monitor's 'key functions' listed in the document is 'promoting competition'.[24] But is the individual really set free by being left to the devices of the market and its largely unaccountable participants? Or are we being subjected to yet another neoliberal social experiment hard on the heels of the failure of the last one, the unregulated market demanded by casino/no-rules capitalism?

There is an unmistakably messianic tone to those touting the market's virtues, and 'Equity and excellence' certainly shares in this, promising to correct the failings of the past and take us into a bright new future where competition for health services will provide us with a radically improved set of services that will transform our lives. But that is what neoliberalism promised us the financial markets would deliver if only we would give them their head and trust in their self-correcting powers, in the actions of rational investors rather than political micromanagement and bureaucratic control. Overall, there is something distasteful about regarding our health problems as products like credit derivatives to be hawked around to profit-obsessed buyers looking for a good return on their investment – not just distasteful, but inhuman in the way it reduces us to mere sources of profit. No amount of rhetorical emphasis on patient choice can overcome that; applying market principles to something so personal as our health demeans us, as if we were *homo economicus* right down to our most basic cell functions. And it seems positively perverse to want to encourage diversity of service provision within the NHS when even defenders of the American system, such as David M. Cutler, concede that it is the presence of such diversity that prevents American healthcare from making the most of the undoubted quality and professionalism at its disposal, leaving so many Americans cast 'adrift'. Diversity has its role in a democracy, but it is by no means a universal good: sometimes it just means confusion.

So should we assume there is a plot being conducted against the NHS? Colin Leys and Stewart Player are firmly of the opinion that there is, and their book by that name is a fierce polemic against what they consider to be the dismantling of the system by means of 'behind-the-scenes lobbying and fixing by a network of insiders', amongst whom they include officials in the Department of Health and a clutch of corporations desperate to get their hands on the trade currently locked up in the NHS.[25] Leys and Player outline a history of tinkering with the NHS going back to the Thatcher government in the 1980s, whereby elements of privatisation are gradually introduced until the operations of the system are more in the private realm than in the public. They catalogue a long list of government-initiated consultations with the private sector that have brought the organisation to the brink of full-scale privatisation, and are scathing of the evidence that has been cited by representatives of the private sector during these consultations to prove its overall greater efficiency, claiming that it is either selective or openly misleading: 'the fact remains that all the evidence shows that privatisation makes health care more costly – and worse'.[26] To opt for the American model is for the authors to choose the worst of all possible worlds that are open to healthcare.

Tempting though it is to regard such a 'plot' as party-political, the narrative provided by Leys and Player makes it clear that the NHS is in the awkward position that it is now because governments on both sides of the British political divide have been committed to the notion of privatisation for quite some time. Any difference between them has been largely a matter of degree rather than of kind: since the 1980s there has been steady progress towards turning the NHS into at the very least a public–private cooperative venture. Neoliberal ideology, in other words, has won the day, and no one in British government circles over the past thirty years or so has been disputing its principles, only the extent to which these are applied and how fast the timetable should be. The coalition government has decided this should be flat out, and 'Equity and excellence' represents a significant move towards meeting the wishes of the Independent Healthcare Association that eventually 'the NHS would simply be a kitemark attached to the institutions and activities of a system of purely private providers'.[27] Who elected the Independent Healthcare Association executives, one might ask, that they could be involved in such a momentous change to British social and political life? The point needs to be reiterated that even if the coalition government backs down on some of its more radical proposals for the NHS, groups like the Independent Healthcare Association will still be there on the sidelines, campaigning away relentlessly and just waiting for the next opportunity that comes along to extend the reach of privatisation for their collective benefit.

Although the majority of the NHS's professional ranks have remained steadfast in their commitment to the organisation and its aims, thirty-odd years of government changes and propaganda on behalf of private healthcare have produced some converts, or 'doctorpreneurs' as they have been dubbed. As Leys and Player remark, 'according to several private health industry journals, many GPs are becoming increasingly entrepreneurial in spirit, having "seen the writing on the wall"'.[28] What that writing reveals is that there is serious money to be made by getting into the private sector at such a critical time when radical change is generating sudden opportunities for those with the right expertise. That is a category including politicians, several of whom have moved from negotiating with private companies over healthcare change to lucrative consultancy and directorship roles within the private sector. While this appeal to humankind's greedy side has worked in some cases, what is perhaps most striking is that the neoliberal ethic has been rejected by so many of the NHS's professionals, and the NHS Consultants' Association (NHSCA) has consistently spoken out against the moves being made towards privatisation.[29] For the time being anyhow, doctorpreneurs are in the minority.

The NHS can certainly be improved, and like any large-scale system it can be bureaucratic and sometimes fail to live up to its highest standards: mistakes can happen, wastage of resource can occur, some sections of the staff can become set in their ways and resistant to even small changes in practice. But the idea that such problems would never arise under a privatised regime is just an illusion; the many scandals in which private healthcare companies in the USA have been involved over the years, and particularly of late, should be enough to signal this. As Leys and Player point out, 'Healthcare markets offer huge scope for fraud and other kinds of malpractice. In the US overcharging, failing to honour insurance policies, late payments of insurance claims and other kinds of malpractice are widespread.'[30] There is no reason to believe that we will not have to face up to similar sharp practice becoming the norm in the UK if we continue on down the privatisation route at the speed we are currently being propelled. From a European standpoint, American healthcare looks like something of a lottery, and if anything there is even greater potential for bureaucracy in the negotiations between the patient, the medical establishment, the insurance company, and state laws, the 'obstacle course' bemoaned by Cutler. The latter's point about the substantial overspend in American healthcare also needs to be emphasised as much as possible: how often have you ever heard an advocate of the American system mention that detail? We should be asking why we are being asked to move closer to a system that can both overspend but fail to provide any coverage at all to 15 per cent of its population. The answer, of course, is profit; but we should never accept that in such a critical area of human existence as this.

Conclusion

Where the main problem lies in this debate between public and private is in regarding healthcare as a consumer product, as if it were the same as shopping for food, clothing, computers, cars, or luxury goods. In those cases one can shop around and compare prices, perhaps even decide not to buy anything at all. The only time that healthcare might conceivably approximate to consumer shopping is when it concerns self-enhancing cosmetic surgery; that is, procedures not required by injuries, such as disfiguring burns or scars. Facelifts and breast enlargements, for example, truly qualify as elective procedures because neither your physical nor psychological health is at risk if you decide not to opt for these after all. It is noticeable in this respect that cosmetic surgery is an area in which the private health system tends to specialise, and there is no doubt that it can be a considerable money-spinner, attracting a wealthier clientele who can afford to indulge their whims in this fashion, to exercise 'choice' over their appearance. No doubt, too, that we can expect to see more and more of such treatments on offer as the private sector expands its services in the UK. Treatment for sickness is a need, however, not a 'want' along the lines of self-enhancing cosmetic surgery. It is little short of grotesque to think of individuals being expected to shop around to find the best deal on heart surgery or cancer treatment as if these were no different than aesthetic decisions about their looks. Reducing serious medical conditions to marketing opportunities has to count as an affront to our humanity; perhaps nowhere else is the insidious effect of the profit motive more clearly revealed than over this.

Neoliberals just cannot seem to see life in any other way than as a series of financial transactions between individuals, a perpetual round of buying and selling. Everything is a potential product and there would appear to be no area of your life into which they believe the market cannot be introduced – and anywhere it has not yet been introduced is just asking to be opened up to the profit motive. Healthcare is being targeted by neoliberals as an area ripe for development, therefore, particularly in countries like the UK where the private sector has played such a minor role since the foundation of the NHS in the 1940s. All that the neoliberal lobby can see there is a large and as yet relatively untapped market that will be a reliable source of profit into the indefinite future, illness always being with us. There is nothing remotely philanthropic or social-minded about their interest, no matter how many smiling faces of apparently satisfied customers you may see on their promotional literature or websites to give that impression. Education is another area that is increasingly being targeted by that sector for the same reasons, as I shall now go on to investigate next.

9
Education and Profit: The World of Pay-as-You-Learn

Higher education has been another area in the UK and Europe which has been under considerable pressure from government in recent years to move from a largely publicly funded to privately funded basis. Students in the UK, as well as elsewhere in Europe, are now saddled with course fees at university, something unknown to previous generations of UK graduates such as my own. In the UK these fees have been increased to a level that may well price many people out of higher education altogether, and both the general public and the lecturing profession have expressed considerable disquiet over this. Already it has forced many in the student body into time-consuming part-time work that could have an adverse effect on their studies.[1]

Governments now insist that the only real value of higher education is economic, arguing, for example, that increased fees should be viewed in the context of the increased lifetime earnings the graduate is likely to experience, thus to be a debt worth incurring: a case of what has been dubbed 'pay-as-you-learn'. The notion of self-development, through education, as a public good effectively has been hijacked in favour of self-development as the means to more individual earning power. So welcome to the world of pay-as-you-learn, with its clear implication that learning is essentially a financial transaction, just another product offered for sale by a consumer society.

What the longer-term effect of this policy on higher education in countries like Britain might be is hard to determine as yet, although there are already fears being voiced that it may lead people away from the humanities and social sciences to more obviously vocational subjects where jobs and careers can be more or less guaranteed and loans therefore repaid more easily. But it unquestionably provides further reinforcement for a profit-centred ideology, as it is intended to do. Knowledge is now only treated as a public good as long, and only as long, as it is a source of economic profit, and that is a desperately reductive view of the human condition which needs to be resisted as strongly as possible from the grass roots upwards. If we are now in an economic depression thanks to the irresponsible actions of a financial industry putting immediate profit above all else, and most notably the public good, then the same mindset may well be leading us into an equally problematical 'educational depression' – the possible landscape of which will be discussed later in the chapter. It is instructive to compare the American higher educational system with the British in order to assess whether the former can be taken as a model for how the latter should develop, as right-wing politicians in the UK increasingly like to claim, or whether the extent of the cultural differences between the two countries would make this not just difficult but possibly even undesirable.

The Educational Market

It is invariably America that is held up as a model for the British university system, despite the major cultural differences that exist between the two countries, which have a very different kind of social history behind them and thus very different expectations of institutions and their role. There is a general agreement amongst educationalists that American universities are amongst the world's very best, and places like Harvard, Yale, and MIT are internationally renowned, and deservedly so, for the quality of the educational experience that they provide. As Jonathan Wolff has pointed out, 'all surveys suggest that around 75% of the world's best universities are in the US'.[2] The elite American universities are invariably also richer than their British counterparts enabling them to spend far more on their research culture, and through that investment to become world leaders in many fields, particularly in the sciences, where they excel. One of the arguments given for raising fees by several hundred per cent in British universities is that they need the extra income thereby generated to compete with their American counterparts, particularly on the research front, and that if this is not forthcoming then they will slide into the second division of the university world internationally with a consequent knock-on effect on their future prospects. High-flying students and researchers will then go elsewhere that can offer them higher quality, and with it improved career opportunities, which most likely will mean the USA rather than the UK. The market, in other words, will turn against the UK.

What is left out of account in such arguments is, in the first place, the sheer diversity of the American university system, which varies far more on a quality index than the British one does. Not every American university is Harvard, Yale, or MIT, although that tends to be the impression given by British advocates of the American system, who use those institutions and their ilk as the standard measuring device. What is also left out of account is, as was alluded to earlier, the degree of cultural difference that obtains. America is a far richer country overall than Britain, by any standard of gauging per capita wealth and gross national product, and university alumni find it correspondingly easier to make substantial endowments to their alma mater. British universities simply do not have the same reservoir of wealth to tap into because of that, and the fact that the alumni system is nothing like as well developed here does not help matters either. There is a considerable cultural difference between the countries in this respect, that encourages all American graduates, even those not at the high end of the income scale, to feel under an obligation to contribute. Neither are British universities as market-oriented in going about exploiting what is there in the alumni system as the Americans clearly are. It would require a fairly radical change of mindset within the system to start regarding alumni financial contributions as a critical activity; in effect, the university's life-blood, an income stream without which it would soon slide into decline, or even go out of business entirely. While there is some activity of this kind taking place within the British system, the fund-raisers themselves would have to become far more aggressive if they were to begin to match their American peers – a trait that does not come as easily to Europeans as it does to Americans, much though our political masters might wish it would.

One recent case indicates the difficulties that can arise when universities find themselves pressurised into fund-raising in order to maintain their international profile, and that concerns the London School of Economics (LSE) and the Libyan government of Colonel Gaddafi. The LSE forged close links with the Gaddafi regime which have been financially very beneficial for it. Gaddafi's son, Saif al-Islam, read for a doctorate there and then made a donation of £1.5 million to the institution; a donation which the students' union even supported the receipt of as opening up a potential route to exercising a positive influence on a regime internationally notorious for its cynical attitude to human rights. A deal was also struck to train up 400 'future leaders' of Libya in management and leadership skills: this netted the LSE a further £1 million in fees. Once revolution broke out against the Gaddafi regime in 2011 and the West collectively turned against him, the LSE was left in such an embarrassing position as an apparent supporter of the now rapidly discredited regime that its director, Sir Howard Davies, felt compelled to resign. The fact that Saif al-Islam's doctorate has subsequently been the subject of allegations of plagiarism from various quarters only adds to the institution's embarrassment. The irony of the situation is that the LSE has been doing exactly what successive British governments from Margaret Thatcher onwards have repeatedly been urging higher educational institutions to do: to get out there in the wider world and sell themselves as hard as they can, to turn higher education into a source of profit.

Other British companies had been dealing with the Gaddafi regime for quite some time, with government approval, so one possible line of defence is that the LSE was merely following a well-established trend in the business world. And other British universities were also setting up their own deals with the regime that are now slowly coming to light as the press follows up the story, much to the universities' embarrassment even if they were entered into with good faith at the time. But the crucial difference between an educational institution and a standard business is that educational 'products' (that is, degrees and qualifications) are not mere artefacts to be bought and sold on the open market, they have to be earned by the individual – without reference to that individual's social status or funding source. It may well be that the doctorate gained by Saif al-Islam Gaddafi was genuine, but the suspicion of special treatment continues to linger with any such arrangements that universities enter into. Can a university reasonably enough fail students who come in a package deal like that with the 'future leaders'? The chances are that if they do then the country involved will simply shift to a different institution. This is of course standard business practice, you can always take your custom elsewhere if you are dissatisfied in any way with the service you receive when buying your 'product'.

Questions are now being asked about deals the University of St Andrews has entered into with the regime in Syria (also in the process of being ostracised by the West), so the Libyan case is by no means a one-off. Yet the more that higher education is drawn into this policy then the more exposed it will become to the kind of scandals of sharp practice that regularly shake the business world, and its integrity will just wither. What universities must always remember is that their products only have the 'value' they do because they are deemed to be above the commercialism of the business world; when that ceases to apply then no one will trust degree certificates any longer, and that will be a sad day if it ever arrives.

The internal market has now become a factor in the British university system, and it can lead to some strange practices being tried out, that demonstrate only too clearly how the internal market can distort academic life, and indeed actively hinder it in the pursuit of its traditional goals. If, for example, university courses are costed according to how much staff time they take to deliver, and if the staff of other faculties within the same university are brought in to do some of the teaching, then it makes sense for that other faculty to charge for its own staff's time for outside-faculty work. This represents additional money that the other faculty has to find, depleting its annual budget to the benefit of the faculty whose staff is being 'loaned out'. One way out of this dilemma is to hire part-time staff to do the needed teaching instead, since they cost less per hour than full-time staff do. In theory the faculty saves money, therefore: part-time staff simply cost less per hour, so your outgoings drop. But if the faculty is making a saving, the university as a whole is not, since the full-time staff who are prevented from teaching in another faculty than their own are still being paid their full salaries. The ultimate logic of this policy would be to keep full-time staff to a minimum and convert the bulk of your teaching to part-time, which some institutions might well wish to do to improve their financial position. On the intellectual side something is being lost too, the opportunity to develop interdisciplinary work that may open new lines of research and generate interesting new programmes for students. It is all so short-sighted, and inimical to the best traditions of the academic world, which has always thrived on intellectual cooperation; but it means that the internal market can be claimed by management to be in force, thus keeping their political masters happy.

Another example of the new accounting that the internal market has brought into play is that all rooms are now costed against designated 'cost centres', such as faculties, which can on occasion result in academic conferences being priced out of the institution where they have been developed because it is too expensive to hire the rooms that are needed. It is hard to see who gains from this, since intellectual debate and the sharing and dissemination of knowledge are supposed to be at the heart of a university's mission; one would think that anything that inhibited the realisation of these objectives would be avoided. The notion that rooms constitute profit sources as opposed to just teaching facilities can even lead to faculties being given targets by the university central management for letting them to outside agencies, such as commercial companies, out of teaching hours – nights, weekends, holidays, etc. This in turn can lead faculties to expect their teaching staff actively to seek outside potential sources of income in this way.

At one time the carrot offered by university managements for engaging in such non-academic activities was that any extra income made through them would be ploughed back into research funding, rendering academics' lives easier on that score at least. Earn money, win research leave; so went the equation. That notion tends to have been overtaken, however, by the more general university need to show a profit on its activities overall, therefore to hang on to whatever extra income is generated by its staff, at whatever activity. Managers desperate to balance the books have increasingly been driven to adopt policies of this kind. Everyone in the system is under the same pressure these days, and it is becoming more insistent year by year. Money is always in short supply in this sector, and it is likely to get ever shorter in the immediate future.

Even research is now caught up on this treadmill, being expected, even required, to yield a profit: indeed, subjects which fail to do so, or even earn what their institution considers to be an insufficient amount from their research efforts, can find their very existence under threat, with many such already having been closed down for precisely that reason. While the creation of profit is always a possibility in the sciences, research findings frequently having technological application which companies can be only too keen to get their hands on for commercial exploitation, it is much harder to achieve in the arts and humanities. The upshot has been a fair amount of soul-searching amongst arts and humanities staff to justify the continuation of research activity, which rarely will prove to have any direct financial outcomes, certainly not on the scientific model. Profit here is interpreted in the most narrow fashion, as is the current wont, as financial profit.

The profit mentality is now so well embedded in the system that it confronts the individual academic at almost every turn. Academics do not like it, and few become academics with this goal in mind; but presumably that will have to change as income generation becomes part of the initial selection process for academic posts, as is indeed already happening in the UK in the humanities. It is now a key factor when it comes to promotion, with research reputation amongst one's peers no longer counting as enough on its own to merit this: poor performance on the income generation front is bad news for your career prospects. Neither will it come as a surprise to learn that it is increasingly becoming a critical factor in academic performance-pay schemes too, another area of much contention.

Another worrying trend is for the business world to become much more active in higher education, to the extent of sponsoring programmes at existing institutions, running in-house post-experience courses on their own premises, validated by accredited institutions, and even exploring the setting up and operating of their own institutions of higher education. This is a development which is unlikely to meet with much opposition from most governments in the prevailing climate. The UK government is in fact planning to facilitate expansion in this area, and is introducing legislation to this effect. The objective, as the government sees it, is to create more diversity in the higher education sector. Business leaders are already very vocal in demanding that universities turn out graduates with the skills they most value, and complaining that the current system is failing to meet their needs. Arts and humanities graduates are not what the business world wants, not unless they have been given a thorough grounding in such things as entrepreneurialism and management skills as well. Topics of that kind are creeping onto the syllabuses more and more in the arts and humanities area as universities succumb to persistent official pressure to ensure that all their graduates have 'transferable skills' to take with them into the world of employment – and such skills are beginning to revolve, not unexpectedly given the political climate, around the notion of entrepreneurialism.

Discussions are already under way, therefore, to grant credit status towards a degree for in-house training in the corporate world, which would of course be a big money-saver for central government were it to take off in any big way. Even if the government were to provide some subsidy at first, as seems likely it would in order to get the schemes off the ground and encourage corporations to participate, this would amount to less than funding actual universities; although whether it would continue to represent a saving overall in the longer term would have to remain a moot point. Apart from anything else it might end up costing individual students more in fees than the current system does, as private providers sought to maximise their profit margins, as private companies invariably will. This would amount to outsourcing university education, a policy which governments are increasingly committed to with public services in general. If rubbish collection and hospital cleaning and portering services can be outsourced, then why not teaching as well?

The monitoring body for higher education in America, the US Higher Learning Commission (HLC), has found itself with its hands full in recent years dealing with the increasing problems arising in the for-profit branch of the sector. One of its most recent investigations has been into Apollo Global, an education multinational that owns private universities in various American states, as well as in Puerto Rico, Mexico, Chile, Canada, the Netherlands, and now the UK in the form of BPP University College. The Commission has launched an inquiry into Apollo's 'recruiting, admissions and financial aid practices' in its American operations, claiming that the company has been deceiving students.[3] Apollo has a record of dubious practices behind it, having already been convicted of securities fraud, as well as charged by the US Department for Education with withholding a critical report on its activities from its shareholders. Having been placed in an extremely awkward position by this embarrassing turn of events, Apollo's British outpost, BPP University College, which it had acquired in a takeover in 2009, has tried to placate fears with a public statement by its chief executive that:

> We are a degree awarding body [power to do so having been granted by the Department of Business, Innovation and Skills in 2007] which

means we have a much tougher regulatory regime applied to us and a much different regime to that in the United States. I run the UK operation, BPP, which is entirely run by the UK team and has no direct control from the United States, and we are under the UK regulatory regime.[4]

Whether BPP can remain completely uninfluenced by its parent company's policies would have to be a moot point: that is hardly the standard way of the business world after all. It is already bearing out one of the main fears of opponents of the private system, however, in that it is restricting itself to subjects that will wear higher fees: business studies (particularly financial practice) and law, both of which, in theory at least, can lead to high-paying careers afterwards. It is just such cherry-picking that worries those in the public sector, who are still expected to offer coverage across the discipline spectrum, which is much more expensive to do.

BPP bears out yet another fear that has been voiced, that such institutions will be very vulnerable to corporate takeovers, which is hardly a recipe for stability or continuity. To the corporate world education is just another source of revenue; they are unlikely to be going into it for any high-minded reasons. Neither are corporations accountable to the general public for their actions, only to their shareholders. That set-up means that the public has no real say in what takes place in a private university, except in the crude sense of withdrawing its custom if dissatisfied. The point should be made also that if we are willing to allow this to occur at higher education level, then there is no good reason why it should not be made to apply throughout the whole of the educational process.

There is absolutely no pedagogical reason to encourage private higher education in the UK. There is no proof that UK universities are systematically failing their students, nor that they are offering a substandard product. Criticisms of that nature would only be valid if you thought that entrepreneurialism should be the primary outcome of university study in any subject. Neither is there evidence to suggest that the first private university to open in the UK, the University of Buckingham, is outperforming the public sector. The decision to push the private is purely ideological, based on the premise that market competition must be present in every area of our lives, and that profit really does guarantee our independence. If Apollo Global is anything to go on, however, the profit mentality is just about the last thing that we need more of in the higher education sector.

Educational Depression?

I floated the term 'educational depression' earlier: what might this be like? Let us say that the current policies did lead in time to a massive turning away from the arts and humanities to the hard sciences: how would this change our society, and would that change be for the better or the worse? This would seem to be what most governments want, more science graduates; the belief being that science holds the key to our economic future, so the more of us engaged in it the better. Science equals improved technology from this viewpoint, and improved technology means above all more profit, especially if you can steal a march on your national competitors in the global market with some new cutting-edge product and/or system. Few governments are willing to invest in the arts and humanities because they cannot see any direct economic benefit arising from them; as a recent newspaper editorial on educational policy summed it up quite bluntly, current policy 'puts in jeopardy subjects like, say, archaeology or philosophy that enhance what it means to be human without necessarily contributing to GDP'.[5] Contribute or die – or at the very least, contribute or deserve to die – would seem to be the directive coming from central governments.

GDP or not, however, it is nevertheless the case throughout most of the Western world, and certainly in the UK, that the arts and humanities are becoming ever more popular with students, far outstripping science subjects in recruitment terms. The bulk of the expansion of the university population in the last few decades has in fact come in the arts and humanities, the opposite of what the political class really wants and what it thought expansion would deliver when it started pushing the idea of mass higher education a few decades back. Politicians and the public are clearly out of step on this issue, particularly, as mentioned above, in the UK, where the public is repeatedly voting with its feet no matter what exhortations the government may make about the need for greater numbers in science and engineering. Most higher educational establishments in the UK would hardly function at all were it not for the strong presence of the arts and humanities within them, and this is despite the fact that the money coming in to fund research is overwhelmingly for the sciences at the expense of arts and humanities subjects. Science subjects are also receiving much higher per-capita fees from government for teaching purposes, which managements are always extremely keen to access. Money is rarely grudged for high-profile science research projects, but it is hard to find in even small amounts, compared with the scale of science budgets anyway, for all the other disciplines that go to make up academia.

However, let us imagine that the arts and humanities actually did begin substantially to decline, that public funding was systematically withdrawn, and that the sciences came to dominate the university landscape in recruitment terms: how might this affect our culture in a general sense? The argument from the arts and humanities side has to be that we would be all the poorer for the loss of the ideas that flow from this sector, not to mention the more practical point that standards might well go down in areas like art, writing, music, theatre, and the performing arts in general. The argument back from the science obsessives is that these are peripheral activities in an advanced society, and that if people really want to engage in them then they will do so whether or not there is public financial support forthcoming. To be fair, this has been the pattern over much of human history, where any patronage that has existed has been at best erratic. Whether that is an argument for continuing in that way is another question; after all that has also been the case with science funding and no one is suggesting that should still apply in an advanced society. The science obsessives are not against the arts and humanities as such, they just do not regard them as anything much other than leisure-time pursuits that the public can either support at a private level, out of their own pockets and spare cash, or not, as they wish: Friedman would undoubtedly agree.

The private sector might take up the slack for arts and humanities subjects, as it is beginning to do in other areas at the moment, but only for a fee, which would of course be subject to the profit motive. How competitive they would be in cost terms remains to be seen, but one suspects they would aim for the higher income brackets where spare cash was more readily available, which would run the risk of overcoming all the good that has been done in recent decades in widening participation in higher education to those from a lower socio-economic group background. Specialised operations like BPP University College give us an idea of where this is most likely to lead. The next issue would be that of quality control and whether that could be maintained at the current exacting standards of the publicly funded system. Profit will always be short-term in its outlook, not long-term and speculative, and that will never be good news for higher education. Opting for short-termism in this way might perhaps be seen as an example of the automatic brain triumphing over the controlled. The stories coming out of America about the private universities there do not bode well at all in this respect; surely we cannot assume that an organisation like Apollo is the face of the future in higher education?

I am not arguing against the sciences, nor am I underestimating their importance to our culture. The problem is rather that they are seen to be essential to the national welfare, while the arts and humanities are considered to be sidelines only, areas that, unlike science, we could live without if we had to. Clearly, artists, writers, musicians, etc. will continue to come forward even if their subjects begin to slide down the university pecking order. Not all of them are university graduates in our own day anyway, nor need they be. The more intensely and intensively those kind of subjects are taught and studied, however, then the more they are seen to be central to our lives, and, one would hope, the more professional, socially conscious, and open to new ideas they become. Take that resource away, or reduce it really substantially, and you are likely to diminish the standing of the arts in the public eye, as well as making it more difficult for creative artists to make a living out of their art alone, or to obtain the kind of professional training that would speed up their development.

It is also questionable whether science can do without the arts and humanities, whether it is quite as self-contained an area as its believers think. Ideas can come from anywhere, and science has drawn fruitfully on disciplines like philosophy, to name an outstanding example, over the years. Scientists themselves are less likely to view their subject as a discrete area of enquiry than their politically motivated supporters are, and are generally well aware of their interaction with other disciplines and how both sides gain from it. It is well known how influenced by science and its theories the arts have been over the years, but it should be recognised that the traffic is two-way. It is not just social life that would be the poorer were the arts and humanities to be driven into decline, but scientific life as well. One would hope that it was recognised by those in power that the more ideas there are around in a society, then the more likely it is that everyone, scientists included, will benefit from the resulting intellectual ferment. Science may be highly specialised, but it is not separate from the rest of life.

We might well ask, too, what would happen if the critical disciplines were to lose public funding and be left to the mercies of the market. One would have thought that it was self-evident what the virtues of a critical temperament are to an advanced society like ours: the more of that temperament and cast of mind there is around then the less likely it is that society will fall victim to prejudice, authoritarianism, and other such anti-social, and anti-civilising, phenomena. We know from experience how easy it is for these attitudes to take root so the more scrutiny that our institutions, politicians, and business world are permanently under the better, and this is at least in part achieved by the development of critical studies in our educational sector. Our rulers do *not* always know best: democracy has far more need of critical minds than of neoliberalism.

The political obsession with science does keep coming to the fore, however: just think of all the campaigns to boost science study that there have been in recent decades, all of them seeing it as imperative to the nation's future that the area expand rapidly. Yet an arts and humanities-light, science-heavy university sector is not the way to improve our society, no matter how much our political class may believe it is. That would indeed constitute an educational depression: a world in which the arts and humanities were at best tolerated and left to the whims of the market for their survival, rather than enthusiastically supported and given official recognition as an important, indeed no less essential than the sciences, part of our lives.

A recent initiative shows a welcome recognition of the need to take some action to arrest the erosion of arts and humanities' provision in UK higher education, if also of the drawbacks of having to do so in the current political climate. The eminent British philosopher A. C. Grayling is setting up a new venture called the New College of the Humanities, which plans to charge double the present maximum fees allowed for degree-awarding institutions in the UK. It promises to be staffed by an impressive array of celebrity academics: Richard Dawkins, Niall Ferguson, Steven Pinker, for example. While the impulse behind this is probably high-minded, it merely serves to entrench the pay-as-you-learn market model ever more firmly into the public consciousness, especially with fees of £18,000 per year as a starter. Fees at that level will be a deterrent to all but the well-off, and although a system of scholarships has been promised, it remains to be seen whether this will reach out much past middle-class students. One suspects that the government will be quite happy to see initiatives of this kind coming forward, showing a willingness to embrace the American elitist system and to stand or fall on one's marketing abilities, as the new college would be obliged to do. Even the parliamentary opposition has offered a guarded welcome to the plan, while bemoaning the fact that such an initiative has become necessary to protect something so intrinsically worthwhile. If the government itself had suggested double fees for studying the arts and humanities there would have been a public outcry, but when a group of big-name academics do so then it sets a precedent: yes, you can still study the arts and humanities, but at a cost. Critics have not been slow to come forward from within the profession, however, and Grayling can expect to hear a lot more from them as his plan takes shape.

No doubt others will follow this precedent, but that will edge us ever further towards an entirely private system which privileges the rich able to afford the fees to study under the intellectually famous. That runs the risk of creating a cultural elite similar to the political elite that is produced by Oxbridge, hardly a very democratic outcome. Grayling himself nevertheless seems to think it is inevitable that others will follow his lead: 'Other universities might also think "either we sink or go independent".'[6] That brings us right back to the equation made by James Murdoch between profit and independence, and indeed the report on the initiative notes that, '[i]t is set up to deliver a profit to its shareholders who include the professors and a team of wealthy businessmen who have bankrolled the plan.'[7] It's that dread word 'profit' again, as if providing an educational service were unthinkable without it. Celebrity academics might do very well out of this, assuming there are enough of them to go around; but it cannot be seen as the answer to the crisis looming in the arts and humanities, and, indeed, in mass higher education more generally. It's simply another instance of the market dictating the terms on which we must live, and when it is let loose on such activities as this its effect is to increase elitism in our society. Who knows, perhaps the next step will be hospitals staffed with celebrity doctors?

What Price Research?

I will end this sortie into the educational world of pay-as-you-learn by returning to the question posed by John Parrington, pertinently enough a scientist at Oxford University, to provide evidence for the assertion just made that practising scientists do not necessarily share the tunnel vision of their government advocates: 'how can money be used to assess a valuable new insight into Shakespeare as he wrote his plays, or the social changes that led to the first flowerings of democracy in Ancient Greece?'. It is precisely such questions that arts and humanities academics in the UK find themselves being forced to come up with answers for in these days of government-generated research assessment exercises, and, yes, answers can be manufactured, although they involve giving in to the game that your profit-obsessed political masters are forcing you to play. Books on Shakespeare sell and make money for the publisher, as do books on Greek civilisation; television spin-offs may occur in such cases, which can be sold to overseas markets or bring in advertising revenue at home. The real point, however, is that the value of such research is other than financial, especially in the crude sense in which it is being interpreted by government auditors: one might as well ask if attending a Shakespeare play yields profit, or voting in an election or exercising any other of your democratic rights. The value is to be judged in terms of our quality of life, that most amorphous yet also most prized of entities, and that can never come with a price tag attached to it – although increasingly that is what neoliberals are insisting upon, as we have become only too well aware when it comes to education and healthcare. There is a confusion of categories taking place here: a lifestyle and the financial activities that people engage in within it are not equivalent and cannot necessarily be judged according to the same criteria. The former encompasses the latter and not the other way around. Next, let us to turn to yet another category confusion, the last of the volume's case studies, the world of the arts and profit.

10

The Arts, the Media Industries, and Profit

A nother victim of the post-credit crunch enthusiasm for cuts in public spending has been the world of the arts, which in many European countries has generally been the recipient of quite significant public subsidy and government support in the modern era. The argument for such support has been that the arts are a civilising influence on society that should not just be left to the whims of the private sector – as they still largely are in the USA, for example, where private patronage has to be openly canvassed by arts organisations on a permanent basis, and fund-raising is a big business. Instead, the idea that has grown up in modern times in Europe is that the arts should be fostered, like higher education, for the public good. Although the claim is sometimes made that both the arts and education are largely middle-class preserves, there is still a feeling throughout most of Europe that they must at least be made available to all classes of society and that public funding is the best way to ensure that this occurs. In truth, artists and art-lovers can come from any class of society, and public funding simply makes the arts more accessible to those lower down on the economic scale.

Unfortunately, this idea of the arts as a political responsibility is now being put under considerable strain. Arts organisations in countries like the UK particularly are being asked to emulate the American model of applying for grants and funding from private organisations if they wish to continue operating at the level they have been, and to become far more profit-conscious about their operations into the bargain. The expectation is that in future private patronage, and box-office receipts, will largely replace public subsidy. To this end, government funding for the arts in England, administered through the Arts Council of England (ACE), was cut by 15 per cent in 2011, and the US Senate has cut the budget of the National Endowment for the Arts (NEA) by 14 per cent.

Again, the effect of such a policy change is to reinforce the notion that any human activity can only be justified if it generates profit: aesthetic value is increasingly being equated with economic value, which is surely a tendency that should be spoken out against very strongly. Apart from anything else, the creative impulse is not in the main generated by economic considerations, and it deserves to be nurtured and supported for entirely other reasons. The arts can never be completely divorced from the economic realm: writers, painters, and musicians need earnings to survive, just like the rest of us do. We devalue creative activity quite drastically, however, if we see it only as a route to creating profit, and unworthy of any substantial public support unless it can prove conclusively that it does so. To inject even more of the profit motive into creative activity will be to the benefit of neither the art that is produced under that regime nor our culture in general, and is effectively, as was pointed out in Chapter 3, to do violence to the better parts of our nature. Collectively, the arts constitute an institution that helps to reinforce our Social Brain, and the arguments for doing that are strong indeed.

The media industries also ask to be drawn into this discussion, because there the clash between creativity and the profit motive is particularly sharply felt. Media such as film and television are very expensive to run, requiring considerable capital outlay on staff and resources in order to create their end product: millions of pounds can go into creating television series, and Hollywood films can cost hundreds of millions of dollars to make. Artists, and creative people in general working within this area, are made very conscious of the need to recover this outlay, having to go through profit-minded middlemen if they are to bring their work to general public notice. Failure to make profit for the host medium on any regular basis means that opportunities to work are soon closed off, and this is a system that encourages compromise, not something that creators are generally too happy with, and that can have a detrimental effect on their work. The increasingly beleaguered state of public broadcasting systems such as the BBC, forced to compete with profit-making organisations and permanently vulnerable to ideologically motivated government intervention, also needs to be borne in mind. The BBC may be world-renowned for the quality of its output, and the recipient of an impressive array of awards for this over the years, but one would hardly know it from the severe attack it is being subjected to these days from such as the Murdoch media empire and right-wing politicians, who are inimical to the idea of public service in general. In James Murdoch's worldview, as we have seen, the BBC is an enemy to freedom and independence, practically a threat to our democratic way of life and just asking to be cut down to size on those grounds. The only broadcasters we can really trust, according to Murdoch, are those motivated by profit; which I suspect will come as a surprise to any creative types who have to deal with them on a regular basis, and find themselves having to tailor their efforts to the demands of the market.

Arts Funding in the UK and America

Europe and the USA have, as I've indicated, very different traditions when it comes to funding of the arts. While a certain degree of public funding does exist in America, it is overshadowed by that received from private donations: the NEA budget is only one-fifth of that of the ACE, for example, so the private source is crucial for the survival of the arts in the country. Such donations tend in the main to favour prestigious projects that attract a great deal of public notice, thus enhancing the reputation of the sponsor, which is often a large corporation or multinational mindful of its image. There is, in other words, an agenda at work which does not necessarily have much to do with the aesthetic, more with public relations. Corporations have received tax breaks on donations to the arts since

1936, but it has been estimated that such philanthropy has declined by one-third since 1990, creating considerable difficulties for arts organisations in general across America. It is a decline which has been attributed 'to a shift in private-sector leadership, corporate mergers, globalization, and a narrowing of scope in corporate philanthropy'.[1] Given that the period since 1990 had been one of unprecedented corporate profits up until the post-2007 downturn, all of this hardly bodes well for the future. Arts organisations faced with both falling private and public funding will either have to cut their activities back quite drastically, or tailor their programming to the box office by playing safe in what they offer. Programmers may be able to overcome this by mixing together popular and less well-known or new works, but the bias will definitely be towards the former. In practice this could mean theatres full of revivals of classic hits; concert programmes concentrating even more than they do now on popular works of the past and neglecting new, and difficult, contemporary music; gallery exhibitions of only the stars of the art world; quite probably increased ticket prices to all arts events that cuts down accessibility across the socio-economic spectrum. I intend nothing elitist by such an argument: there is of course nothing wrong in presenting popular works, but the ultimate effect can be to suppress experimentation and make it difficult to extend the range of the arts. If the box office rules altogether, then it is not good news for the arts, which can all too easily stagnate in such conditions.

The current British government is keen to promote the American system as an alternative to public funding of the arts, and particularly its heavy reliance on endowment schemes, where wealthy individuals and companies pledge substantial backing to the institution of their choice over a negotiated period of years. This is not always as effective as its British advocates choose to believe, however, as a recent high-profile case in the USA reveals. The Philadelphia Orchestra, one of the world's leading classical music ensembles with a long and proud history, has filed for bankruptcy in 2011 citing as one of its main reasons for doing so a systematic decline in endowment income – further proof of the general decline noted above. Cuts in funding can happen with public funding too of course, as support for the arts can vary quite considerably between the parties forming the government at any one time: generally speaking, leftist governments are more sympathetic to the arts than rightist. But where public funding is involved at least negotiations can be entered into between the parties and it becomes an issue in the public realm, which governments have to take note of to some extent if they want to avoid bad publicity. No such option is really open in the American system, and the Philadelphia Orchestra has been reduced in this instance to sending a begging letter out to all its patrons in an attempt to stay in existence. This is a humiliating experience for such a famous organisation to have to undergo, and a salutary reminder to their peers of just how precarious their position in society is: if it can happen in Philadelphia then it could happen anywhere. The lesson has to be that private funding is not the universal panacea for the arts that some would like to picture it: endowments, rather like the value of stocks and shares, can go down as well as up.

Profit and Merit

It is entirely possible to argue that, while some individuals do go into the world of the arts with the express intention of making lots of money, the artworks that come out of such a profit-centred initiative are not always very high on artistic merit. There is a well-established 'best-seller' culture in literature, for example, and any product that catches the public mood can shift millions of copies and make millions of pounds, dollars, or euros for both author and publisher. Once such a reputation has been established, extensive advertising playing its part, then the process tends to take on its own momentum and subsequent books by the same author tend to find an audience ready and waiting for his or her latest effort to hit the bookshops. Such work can be of a high order, winning critical as well as popular success, but that is not always the case when a mass market is being aimed at. The aesthetic value of many of the mass-selling books is questionable, and the likelihood is that only a few are likely to be read by future generations in the way that more serious literature, including the acknowledged classics of the world literary heritage, clearly are. There are exceptions: J. K. Rowling is both a critical and popular success, and Booker Prize-winners can sell quite well too. But a more typical example of the mass-seller these days is *The Da Vinci Code*, and one will have to search hard to find a critic willing to make much of a case for that on aesthetic grounds.[2] As far as the commercial publishing industry is concerned, however, a Dan Brown or a Chris Ryan can be as valuable a commodity as a J. K. Rowling: the balance sheet is the bottom line, and commercial merit trumps critical merit.

While it is always difficult to know what generations to come will find aesthetically appealing, books solely written to satisfy the profit motive are very unlikely to have much in the way of lasting qualities, and the same goes with work produced for a similar reason in the other arts. Artists can be as greedy as anyone under the right circumstances, and history provides us with numerous examples. Fortunes can be, and are, made in the arts; but profit is a by-product of artistic success rather than a route to it. If artists are successful then they can become money-conscious and want to make the most of their name while they can: reputations can fluctuate dramatically in the arts and success can be fleeting, so this attitude can be defended up to a point. But that does not mean that artists would give up their art altogether if financial success were not forthcoming. The initial impulse to create is very unlikely to have been set in motion by the profit motive, even if this might kick in over the way to a certain extent as success grows.

Profit or Purpose?

In line with their explorations into altruism in the Social Brain project, as well as their opposition to the *homo economicus* model of humankind, the Royal Society for the encouragement of Arts, Manufactures and Commerce (RSA) has shown an interest in the ideas of the American business analyst Daniel H. Pink, whose concept of the 'purpose motive' is worth exploring with regard to its possible application to creative and artistic work. In his book *Drive: The Surprising Truth About What Motivates Us*, Pink sets out to challenge the notion that it is profit alone that dictates our performance in the workplace, and suggests instead that we are more likely to be motivated if we feel that our work involves 'mastery' and purpose, and where we are given the autonomy to realise these. Mastery is 'our urge to get better and better at what we do' and this offers us a sense of what behavioural scientists call 'intrinsic reward' for carrying out tasks;[3] we do them because they test our abilities and this gives pleasure in itself. Purpose satisfies 'our yearning to be part of something larger than ourselves' when displaying that mastery.[4] Pink feels that employers in general have failed to recognise the importance of such factors to most human beings:

> Too many organizations – not just companies, but governments and nonprofits as well – still operate from assumptions about human potential and individual performance that are outdated, unexamined, and rooted more in folklore than in science. They continue to pursue practices such as short-term incentive plans and pay-for-performance schemes in the face of mounting evidence that such measures usually don't work and often do harm.[5]

Mastery from the point of view of what Pink dubs 'Motivation 2.0' is simply becoming better at what you do for reasons of financial rather than intrinsic reward, with the financial reward providing all the sense of purpose you need;[6] this is the world of performance-related pay schemes and annual bonuses. But Pink believes that there has to be something transcendent about the activity to engage us fully, that money alone will not suffice to bring this state of 'Motivation 3.0' into play.[7] It might be hard to conjure up a sense of something transcendent in absolutely every occupation, many being notably dreary; yet one can see how this would be particularly applicable to the world of the arts. There, it is the activity itself and the artefact that comes out of it that drives the artist; a need for public recognition perhaps, where it is clear that your work and its vision have had an impact on your audience. Or it could be the desire to add to, or challenge, an existing tradition in your field that is the motivating factor. Either way, mastery combines with purpose in carrying through something that is autonomously generated. It is not just a case of making something for sale in the market, with no real concern as to what happens to it after it leaves your hands. Artists care about the effect on the public of their efforts in a way that financial traders never do, but perhaps even more importantly, they draw their intrinsic reward from the act of creativity itself, of experiencing their ideas take shape in whatever their chosen medium may be.

Pink's is a populist account of the phenomena of intrinsic reward and purpose that is very much geared towards helping its readers achieve success in their careers, hence the book's lists of easily digestible bullet points in the stereotypical manner of the business guru. Autonomy and mastery may lead to high levels of performance, '[b]ut those who do so in the service of some greater objective can achieve even more', so their employer would ultimately benefit too.[8] It all depends what 'more' refers to of course: more short-selling or wild risk-taking in the market would hardly be in the public interest, but there is no doubt that Pink's ideas could have wider, and more benign, significance. He points to a rise in volunteerism in the USA as proof that many of us want to move past the personal and contribute 'more' to society at large, for example. Although Pink does not delve all that deeply into the literature of behavioural science, we can draw on the Social Brain project for more substantial evidence of our non-competitive side from the field of neuroscience to back up his claims. Pink's emphasis on the factors of intrinsic reward and transcendent purpose is certainly thought-provoking, and since these can work at both the individual and the group level they become a useful counter to arguments that we instinctively react to all tasks thinking like *homo economicus*, asking: what financial benefit is there in this for me?

The need for a sense of transcendence as well as intrinsic reward in one's work might be seen at work in the acting profession. At the top of the acting tree in financial terms are the Hollywood stars, who can make fortunes out of a successful career, charging millions of dollars for each film in which they appear – hence the hundreds of millions of dollars that blockbusters can cost in production. Careers at this level are often conducted more in the manner of financial traders chasing 'alpha' than creative artists seeking aesthetic fulfilment, and big stars can become fixated on their fees to the exclusion of the artistic side of the enterprise. Many actors undoubtedly aspire to enter into that charmed circle and its opulent lifestyle, but the vast majority know that this is highly unlikely ever to happen to them and are not necessarily all that bothered by the realisation. In fact, at any one time most actors are out of work: competition for parts is fierce and there are always more actors around than parts available for them to play. Nevertheless, the profession continues to expand in numbers, and although some of those entering no doubt are doing so with an eye to hitting the big time eventually, most have other motivations for wanting to act. At least somewhere in that list of motivations is the desire for self-expression and to affect audiences emotionally through the display of one's skill and talent, and the intrinsic reward this brings in combining mastery and purpose will keep the vast majority of actors going throughout a career even if it never yields much in the way of financial success. If it were purely a matter of such reward, the profession would be much smaller: average earnings are not all that impressive, and it is anything but secure as a line of work.

The Media Industries: Profit Versus Purpose

The explosive growth of the media in our time has created a pressing need for content that in principle should be good news for the creative community. Television, radio, and film have a voracious appetite for narrative, especially given the proliferation of channels in the first two areas as broadcasting controls have been relaxed internationally, meaning that writers and actors have more outlets for their efforts than ever before. Much of what is wanted is very formulaic, however, designed to appeal to a popular audience that will draw in advertisers or paying subscribers, so writers in particular may be required to make many compromises, writing to order much of the time. For all the considerable disadvantages that went along with being a writer in the Soviet Union, and thus an employee of the state obliged to make compromises with the party line, having to write for profit was not one of your worries. The tendency in the media, as indicated earlier, is to imitate success and to keep doing so as long as it draws large audiences. In effect, there is a permanent struggle going on between profit and purpose in all the major media, even in the publicly funded ones, which are expected nowadays by governments to compete with their commercial counterparts for audience share in order to justify their existence. Value in the media is equated by owners with profit made from the product put on the market, from either the advertising money generated or audience receipts.

So we find ourselves returning to the problem of how to assess the value of things that undeniably improve the quality of life, when such a category resists being brought within a financial straitjacket and judged by its crude criteria. Totalling up all the money that has changed hands over the years in buying and selling a famous painting – as well as paying to view it in exhibitions and buying in print form for hanging on one's wall, plus all the other spin-offs that great art can be exploited for by the commercial world – tells you nothing at all about its meaning in our lives, nor of the value that we attach to it or the artist culturally. And the same thing goes for all the other arts: is a book to be judged primarily because of its sales, or a piece of music by how many CDs it shifts or how successful it is in attracting paying audiences into concerts? Or Shakespeare by last year's combined box-office receipts? That would be to make a category confusion, assuming that quantity (of profit) is the measure of quality, a confusion that serves to cloud the issue of public funding of the arts in a quite persistent fashion. In this context, we might reflect on Niall Ferguson's comment that, 'I am, unapologetically, as interested in the price of a work of art as in its cultural value.'[9] One can see why this would be so from a historian's perspective, but one also suspects that there is a distinct tendency nowadays to assume that it is the former that determines the latter.

Those who work in the media industries have to deal with this way of thinking on a daily basis, given the intense pressure that there is in this deeply profit-conscious area to deliver 'hits'. Think of how often Hollywood goes for the safe option; thus the spate of remakes, sequels, prequels, and franchise series there has been in recent years. Anything that can build on an established concept that has been proved to work with audiences in the past – *Batman*, *Star Wars*, any number of horror or science fiction movies that go to parts I, II, and III and even beyond, for example – will find it easier to obtain funding than an original project. Or consider also how often successful films are recast as stage plays: a trend that is currently all the rage in both the West End and Broadway, and no doubt elsewhere in world commercial theatre. The equation of value with popularity is hard to miss in such cases, as is the equation of value with profit. The more that public funding for the arts is reduced, and the more it is driven by profit considerations where it does still exist, then the more likely we are to force creative artists into such situations. Some can thrive despite these limitations being in force, but not all can or will, and it hardly encourages anyone to take chances or seek to extend the range of their art.

Advertising is inextricably connected with the media world nowadays and it is an area that draws in creative types, with many well-known film directors having started their careers there. Artists and writers gravitate towards this activity as well, given that it is always on the lookout for new ideas and in recent years has shown itself willing to try more and more extreme ways of catching the public attention, offering wide scope for the exercise of the artistic imagination. One such is what has been called 'guerrilla advertising', using public areas in novel and unexpected ways to promote companies and their products by catching the audience off-guard with a 'narrowcasted' message; although we might reflect on the comments about the role of creativity in this venture made by the author of a book on the topic, Jay Conrad Levinson: 'Guerrillas have only one definition of creativity in marketing: something that generates profits for their business. Big profits? Very creative. No profits? Not creative.'[10] Nothing better sums up the position of creative artists in general within the media machine nowadays: profit is what defines aesthetic value for those who actually run the business, and that is how your work will always be assessed by them, thus determining what your future employment prospects are likely to be.

Conclusion

There never has been a golden age of artistic creativity when artists could work without any concern at all about the financial side of their efforts. Certainly in the modern era there has always been a certain amount of pressure to ensure that they provided what their audiences, and paymasters, were looking for; what might be called the Grub Street phenomenon, where power lies with the business-man and distributor rather than the original producer. But there is undoubtedly more commercial pressure being put on creative artists these days to deliver what the forces of profit demand to fill up their schedules, and also of course to cover their often very size-able operating costs. That has to remain one of the saddest aspects of the dominance of neoliberalism in contemporary culture, its colonisation of the imagination in the name of the profit principle.

11
Conclusion: It Needn't All Be About Profit

Even the most concerted action is not likely to eradicate the profit motive from our lives in the short term, but we can set about devising tactics by which to lessen, and lessen dramatically, the role it is playing in our lives in the longer term; to move us towards anti-profit as a social ideal, to free ourselves from the socially and psychologically stultifying effects of neoliberalism. We are ideologically programmed at the moment to live *for* profit, as if that were our destiny, when what we should be doing is learning to live *with* it, as only one impulse in our character: an impulse that could also be put to far better public use than it is at present in our hyper-possessive individualist culture. It needn't all be about profit therefore. Wealth distribution could most certainly be improved upon, whereas at the moment almost all government attention is on how to facilitate the conditions for wealth generation, as if that alone would resolve all the issues that arise in a democratic society concerning our welfare needs: the Third Way without public funding apparently being the ultimate goal.

The more we realise that we can change our attitude to profit then the more we can explore other ways of providing a focus for our lives. It is entirely possible to live *for* the arts, whether as an artist or an audience member; to accord the arts far higher importance in one's life than wealth, while still recognising the need to make a living and play a productive role in society in doing so. From early schooldays onwards, such ideas can be fostered to encourage a change of attitude about what is valuable in our lives, away from personal financial gain to psychological self-development. Neither do I see this as a case of providing 'bread and circuses' to divert our attention from where power really lies in our society, and how it is being wielded primarily for the benefit of an elite. Rather it is a recognition that for most of us money is in the main no more than a means to an end, and that end is not the making of money for its own sake. Neoliberalism may be fixated on the latter, but our interests are far more diverse than that, and far more likely to involve the exercise of our imaginative and creative abilities, as well as to appreciate the efforts of others more talented in these spheres and to derive more value from that than thinking of new ways to use others to increase our personal profit margins.

It is time to underline how the book's arguments have taken us from dissecting the overweening role of the profit motive in our culture to the position where we can see that we do indeed have the capacity to resist, and significantly reduce, the power it has been exercising over us in recent times: in effect, to tame the profit motive, and the greed it almost inevitably promotes in individuals, in the name of the wider interests of humanity. Faced with the neoliberal monolith, the temptation will be to retreat into our fetish, thinking that we can't really change the system, that it is just too powerful and all-encompassing to be taken on. But that would be a counsel of despair, one we do not have to give in to. Addictions can be cured, cultural paradigms can be challenged and altered, and the first step in doing so is to start talking about them, to itemise their adverse effects, and to picture what life would be like without them – the claims of profit versus anti-profit, growth versus de-growth, and so on. Neoliberalism is never going to be the way to guarantee that society becomes fairer and more just; it is having the opposite effect and progressively widening inequalities, to our general cultural detriment. Unregulated competition is bad for democracy, and so is the suppression of our altruistic tendencies. Most of us do not want to spend our lives striving to assert ourselves in the open market, always on the alert for ways to take advantage of our fellows, no matter how much this may be dressed up as our democratic duty or the highest expression of our faculties. Those who do want to spend their lives that way are not to be treated as role models so much as their antithesis, warnings about what can happen if we suppress our social brain and become one-dimensional personalities who can only see other human beings as there to be used.

The Battle for the Public Sector

As this book has made clear, it is in the public sector where the conflict over profit is at its keenest at present, in areas such as healthcare, education, and council services, and it is likely to remain so for the near future if our political masters are given their way. Profit is attempting to colonise the entire public sector, with the goal of turning as much of it over to private enterprise as quickly as it can: outsourcing is very much the flavour of the times and we already go along with it when it comes to globalisation, so that battle has been part-won. Bit by bit the concept of public service is gradually being devalued, so that the public is made to believe that it is inefficient and costly, and that it will be served far better by the private sector when it comes to any of its general welfare needs. The right-wing press is only too happy to peddle such a message to its readership, and pounces on any failings that ever arise in the public sector as if they were merely the tip of the iceberg for the whole system: here is how your tax money is being wasted. Needless to say, the same claim is never made when any private corporation runs into trouble and fails to uphold its duties to the public; such an event is never taken to be symbolic of the rottenness and inefficiency of capitalism in general, but as an isolated incident. If it were, then the recent near collapse of the Western banking system – only a 'near' collapse because several nation states rescued most of the institutions involved with public money to avoid almost certain social disaster – would have been all the evidence required to prove that this is in urgent need of fundamental, root-and-branch reform. Instead, we now find that the colossal budget deficits run up by saving the financial industry are being laid at the door of certain selected political parties, whose opponents have sold this story to the general public as proof of their competitors' incompetence. It is the fetish at work again: it is simply easier to get our minds around the latter proposition than to face up to the enormity of the former. As a result, apart from the experience of the Netherlands, the banks have had a remarkably easy passage since the crisis, with most governments making no more than token gestures towards reforming them.

One wonders where the evidence for the supposedly superior efficiency of the private sector is to be found, and why the belief in it is quite so widespread. Some private companies are efficient, some are ridiculously inefficient. Professional football clubs in the UK are a glaring example of the latter, with the bulk of them operating on massive, and quite probably unsustainable overdrafts; indeed a sizeable number of them have gone into administration over the past few years, and more are expected to follow in a situation that looks like it has all the makings of a classic case of a financial bubble. Much the same can be said of the public sector: it undoubtedly contains examples of both efficiency and inefficiency in its ranks; although it is probably true to say that the sheer scale of the monitoring and auditing that takes place there nowadays has had the effect of reducing inefficiency over the sector quite markedly. That same kind of monitoring and auditing regime is at best intermittent in the private sector and often does not exist at all: if it did then bubbles would be identified in their infancy and dealt with appropriately. Instead we are asked to rely in the main on that mystical invisible hand of the market correcting problems as it goes.

In retrospect, the banking crisis was a disaster just waiting to happen, since the financial industry was operating in an environment with minimal regulation. 'Liberating' markets had long since become the political order of the day in the West, and the supposed route to even greater economic success than we had been experiencing. That was a state of affairs inviting greater and greater risks to be taken in the pursuit of the great god profit, and the industry duly obliged. The result of such increasingly frenzied speculation was one of the most spectacular bubbles of modern times that threatened to bring down the entire global banking system. There was no sign of the invisible hand to be found at work here, and the spectre of this event continues to haunt us several years later. Liberation effectively turned into anarchy. Financial commentators are even now worrying about the potential building up for yet another dot. com bubble, with many of the new apparent success stories on the Internet looking dangerously overvalued as far as expert opinion is concerned.[1] But as long as corporations are showing a substantial profit – as the banks were, at least on paper – then no one is going to make them see the need for a rethink of their practices or their risk-assessment methods. In such cases, to adapt Žižek slightly, they are too busy 'enjoying' their addiction to take much notice of anything else.[2]

What is all but forgotten in this debate about how best to run public services is why such institutions were set up in the first place: essentially, it was because the private sector was either unable or unwilling to do so, and that it saw its overriding inter-est to be profit rather than improving the living conditions of the public at large. It viewed the public purely as a resource to be used to maximise its profit margins, and took little interest, if any, in the public's general welfare, unless it could be turned into a source of profit in its turn. If the state did not take over, either at national or local level, then public health and safety could not be guaranteed: this was one of the harsh lessons taught Western society by the Industrial Revolution. The welfare state, which all Western nations have developed to a greater or lesser extent, was in part devised as a way of protecting the general public from the excesses of the private sector, whose obsession with profit, as in the initial stages of industrialisation, was despoiling the environment and actively *lowering* the quality of life for most of the population. One only has to read nineteenth-century accounts of city and town life, with its unsanitary slum dwellings, filthy streets, and inadequate rubbish collection and sewage and drainage systems, to realise why public services are necessary and why they should not be left to the mercy of the private sector. The private sector will never willingly become engaged in such activities unless it can see gain, and preferably large-scale gain, easily achievable, to be made; so if it does choose to provide such services it will tailor them for the well-to-do, as happens nowadays with gated communities and their private policing by security firms. We can see where this is probably leading in education too, with the establishment of organisations like the New College of the Humanities, where the lure of the profit to be gained from charging students double the current going rate for a university degree in the UK has brought several wealthy businessmen on board as investors.

When public services are outsourced there is little hard evidence to show that they are more efficient than they were previously. Granted, they are often cheaper overall in terms of their operational costs, but generally only by dint of either cutting corners on the service provided, by significantly reducing staff levels, for example, or by paying much lower wages to their staff than the public service norm. Neither of these policies improves the quality of what is being delivered. You end up instead with disenchanted, unmotivated workers, and higher unemployment levels. In some cases, privatising what was formerly public can end up costing the consumer considerably more. One has only to consider the British railway system, where fares have gone up substantially since privatisation on a system that still is very heavily subsidised by the public purse. In consequence the public is losing both ways, through inflated fares and a higher tax burden. Railway fares in the UK are now among the highest in the world, far higher than those of any of our European competitors.

Outsourcing has hardly been an unqualified success in the prison service either, with numerous embarrassing mishaps to report with the companies involved, such as serious security lapses on several occasions leading to riots and prisoner escapes. Again, any savings made are at the expense of trimming staff wages and thus cutting corners on the service provided wherever possible, one predictable result of which is a high staff turnover that hardly promotes efficiency. Staff loyalty, such as it is, lies with the company employing them rather than with the general public, and that is not a relationship that engenders altruism or a sense of contributing towards a cause that improves the human lot; the cash nexus reasserts itself instead.

So the public sector is now the front line in the struggle between profit and anti-profit, where that conflict is at its starkest and where the stakes are at their highest. The more these services become the remit of a profit-oriented private sector then the greater the risk we run of overall standards declining, and of provision being geared towards the well-off at the expense of the poorer sections of society.

If we were all as naturally competitive as neoliberals claim then it would be extremely difficult to instil any sense of public service in us in the first place; it would simply go against the grain too much, and none but those with poor entrepreneurial skills would be likely to show any interest in such employment. Yet those who work in the institutions of the public sector, such as the NHS, genuinely seem to have developed this trait, and to regard it as a socially worthwhile way to spend their lives – a transcendent factor if you like. If there were no altruistic side to us at all then this would never occur. Opposition from within the NHS, right through its staff levels from support staff to higher management and senior medical personnel, to the policy of hiving more and more of it off to the private sector is always presented by neoliberals as mere resistance to change by those who want to protect their own little sinecures. In reality it stems mainly from a strong sense of pride in what the institution stands for and in the public service that it provides, a public service which is truly democratic. Neoliberals refuse to see it, but it is altruism that is at work here, not self-interest. It is highly likely that senior medical staff could make more money using their skills in the private sector, but most nevertheless stay loyal to the NHS, believing in its mission. Such altruism is widely found throughout the public sector, which attracts people for that very reason. If altruism were really so foreign to our nature and so manifestly against our individual interests then institutions like the NHS would probably never have got off the ground, and certainly never have flourished as it has for so many decades: as noted before, it generates an immense sense of loyalty in its staff that cannot simply be written off as narrow-minded, reactionary resistance to change.

Government policy based on neoliberal principles can certainly block that altruism or make its expression very difficult, but it can never really eradicate it from human nature. The fetish may hide it, but it can never destroy it altogether either; it remains in our social nature.

Institutions like the NHS are in fact testament to just how much of a role altruism plays in our make-up as individuals and how much of a motivation it can be: it seems such a waste to suppress this socially highly beneficial trait. Competition alone would not have brought us to where we are nowadays as a species; that would never have been possible without cooperation, and cooperation requires a strong sense of altruism, of working for the group rather than the individual, the social brain rather than the automatic.

Socialism Versus Profitocracy

I will make a last plea for the revival and redevelopment of a socialist consciousness, because I do not believe we shall realise the potential of our social brain unless we do so, nor become social animals in the fullest sense of the term. Socialism is often attacked for wanting to restrict economic growth, as if that were in some way a betrayal of our nature, as if the profit motive really were encoded in our genes. Hence the tendency of even socialist-minded governments to jump on the neoliberal bandwagon in the last few decades and to jettison many of their founding ideological principles, such as a general commitment to improving the welfare of the collective and reining in individual greed and the unfairness that follows in its wake. The suggestion is that unless there is constant economic growth then we shall all suffer, that prosperity alone holds the key to a better, more fulfilling life for all. It is rule by entrepreneurship. The argument that is often fallen back on in such cases is that restricting growth reduces our ability to improve the human lot through the development of technology, and that we would be turning our back on longer, healthier, and happier lives if we allowed such a policy to prevail. We are to regard ourselves as fortunate to be living in age when we can if we choose, and particularly if we choose neoliberal economics as our guiding principle, promote economic growth and thus bring about all the desirable side effects that it offers. Older generations of humankind did not have that option, and, at least in the mass, lived much more impoverished lives than we do. It is the line taken by such thinkers as Matt Ridley in his book *The Rational Optimist*, where he insists that it is mere stubborn pessimism not to agree with his contention that we live in 'a better today' and should be grateful that we have the means to keep making it even better.[3] Although he is aware that the benefits of 'a better today' are unevenly spread around the globe, the clear message is that we should nevertheless consider ourselves lucky to be living in such an age and that we should therefore put all our faith in the system that has delivered this. In terms of our current world economic order, that means, of course, neoliberalism and the market fundamentalist creed.

One implication of a point of view like Ridley's is that it is economic growth, and the products and benefits that it offers, that is the major determinant of our levels of personal happiness:

> The economist Don Boudreaux imagined the average American time-travelling back to 1967 with his modern income. He might be the richest person in town, but no amount of money could buy him the delights of eBay, Amazon, Starbucks, Wal-Mart, Prozac, Google or BlackBerry.[4]

Another implication is that, if economic growth can be sustained, future generations will be looking back patronisingly on us, wondering how we managed to cope with our inferior technology, relatively primitive medical care, and shorter life-spans. That latter point ought to give us pause for thought, however, because each generation has to cope with life as they find it and not as it might be, otherwise we would be in a permanent state of envy at any one point about what others might come to achieve after us. We should not romanticise the past, but neither should we be patronising towards it. It was entirely possible to lead a happy and fulfilling life before computers, mobile phones, and sophisticated medical care came on the scene – before economic growth of the modern variety occurred either, bringing with it the dubious list of 'delights' just mentioned above. Would it really be such a bad thing if growth stalled, or remained stagnant? Or if we diverted the profits from growth into schemes for improving public welfare, tackling poverty and disease, rather than into the pockets of such individuals as greedy bankers and socially irresponsible entrepreneurs singularly lacking in human feeling and compassion?

Neoliberalism can only drive us further apart as individuals, and will do nothing to nurture the altruism that all societies require if they are to function anything at all like harmoniously. It is an essentially divisive ideology that acts against the impulses of our social brain, and asks us to suppress that side of our character in the name of self-interest, and, ultimately, of profit. Socialism, on the other hand, wants to temper that self-interest and to harness the social brain for the greater public good, to orient us towards the collective rather than the personal. The Big Society, as currently formulated anyway, cannot guarantee a fair and effective system of welfare in the way that a properly run publicly funded one can: Remote Area Medical, for all the good it is undoubtedly doing, is a sign of social failure. Again, a socialist society makes public welfare a priority, doing its best to reduce the number of 'cracks' that people can fall through in the way they manifestly are doing in the American healthcare system, leaving Remote Area Medical and its like to attend to the problems of the developing world, as was its initial intention. Socialism puts its faith in institutions that serve everyone, rather than leaving us at the mercy of entrepreneurs who assume that we are all as profit-obsessed as they are and have as little sense of social responsibility. Entrepreneurs, particularly those who reach tycoon status, are not in fact very representative of society at large; most people are just not interested in devoting their lives to the ruthless pursuit of wealth at the expense of almost all other considerations. Those who reach the rarefied level of international tycoon can seem quite like an alien species to the rest of us most of the time – simply not very rounded individuals, or people we can relate to very well on an everyday human level.

Nor need we accept the argument that democracy can only be guaranteed by the existence of a neoliberal-style free market, and that socialism will always constitute a threat to democracy. Returning to a point I made earlier, I do not see neoliberalism as leading to more democracy but to the establishment of a profitocracy, which is far more of a threat to democracy than socialism ever will be. In a profitocracy there is progressively less public accountability, surely an anti-democratic state of affairs. To whom are shareholders responsible? To no one but themselves and their own self-interest. No one elects shareholders or investors or can turn them out of office if dissatisfied with their conduct, but they have come to exert far more control over our society than politicians in general do, and their collective actions can make or break national economies. We don't elect entrepreneurs or corporate managements either, and if they are accountable at all, then they are only accountable to their shareholders: a closed circle which acts to repel any notion of social responsibility. The idea that we have greater freedom when we let the fortunes of stock markets dictate how the world develops is a complete illusion. To move from democracy to profitocracy is to move from a situation where we have a collective say in how our society operates, to one where we are at the mercy of what looks more like mob action than anything else. Forget neoliberal apologists, markets are just about the antithesis of rationality, and we fool ourselves to think, or be persuaded, otherwise.

Conclusion

It needn't all be about profit, therefore, and it is to curb our potential for self-development, and also for social cooperation and the development of our altruistic tendencies, to believe that it has to be and to remain addicted to that principle, stuck in a neoliberal groove. It needn't be that way and it would be far better for us collectively if it were not. Far better if we offered resistance in some of the forms suggested in Chapter 2: campaigning for consumer boycotts against corporate profiteering and exploitation of developing world labour; campaigning for banks to be turned into public utilities and for privatisation of other public utilities to be reversed; refusing to play the stock market, or at least using our shareholder vote to demand more social responsibility on the part of companies we hold shares in; resorting to whistleblowing to make corporate malpractice public; slowing down the pace of our lives, by, for example, opting out of the 'fast food' culture; opting out of the rat race and reconsidering the whole concept of having a corporate 'career' that dictates our lifestyle; in general, adopting an attitude of principled non-cooperation with the forces of profit and profiteering.

The notion of *homo economicus* does not exhaust our capabilities or our psychological needs, nor is it all that is required to guarantee the continuation of democracy – the example of China alone would serve to dispel such an idea, given that it firmly supports the former but just as firmly resists the latter. And as we have noted, the Murdoch empire is prepared to go along with a state of affairs like that as long as profit is forthcoming. If, as some commentators have been claiming of late, Chinese capitalism really does become the dominant form of that economic system at some point in the near future, then you can bet that the Murdochs of this world will come to an accommodation with it.[5] China already has its own class of entrepreneurs who seem quite content to work within the boundaries of the political system laid down by the country's ruling Communist Party, and although there are dissenting voices within the Chinese system they are not as a rule coming from this class. This is hardly surprising, given that the system is now so heavily weighted towards building up the GDP at the expense of social justice, and so in consequence favours entrepreneurs far more than it does workers, whose rights are fairly minimal.

There may well still be some mileage in exploring the potential of a Third Way, although I think it should take its lead from the social democracy side rather than the personal autonomy one. Few socialists now think that the state holds the answer to everything, or that nationalisation of all key industries and services will resolve all our social and economic problems at a stroke. It is a long way from that position, however, to believing that personal autonomy alone will guarantee our economic security, that we need almost no public sector at all in an advanced society, or that personal autonomy plus profit equals independence. I would be more inclined to say that personal autonomy plus profit equals an increasingly insecure economic environment and a fractious society deeply riven with class divisions. That may suit the likes of James Murdoch and those at the top end of the economic scale with their single-minded commitment to competition, but it does not seem to be what drives the majority of us on a daily basis. At best we are in the mass rather reluctant participants in the neoliberal economic experiment, and it only takes an event like the credit crisis to make us realise just how much of our humanity we have had to give up to keep it going for as long as we have done; hopefully also to question the wisdom of continuing to do so, of remaining in thrall to our fetish on that issue into the future. We only have to think back to the collapse of the Soviet empire to realise that fetishes can be overcome, and that we are under no obligation to go on 'enjoying' our symptom for ever. Life needn't be all about profit, therefore, nor should we allow it to be. Think non-conformity to the current paradigm of unfettered capitalism with its disregard, even contempt, for the general public welfare; think anti-profit and reclaim your sense of humanity by doing so.

Notes

Notes to Chapter 1

1 James Murdoch, 'The absence of trust', 2009 Edinburgh International Television Festival MacTaggart Lecture, 28 August 2009, http://www.guardian.co.uk/media/2009/aug/28/james-murdoch-bbc-mactaggart-edinburgh-tv-festival (accessed 2 April 2011).

2 Susan Strange, *Casino Capitalism*, Oxford: Blackwell, 1986; John Lanchester, *Whoops!: Why Everyone Owes Everyone and No One Can Pay*, London: Penguin, 2010, p. 6.

3 David Cameron, 'Use the profit-motive to fight climate change', *The Observer*, 28 November 2010, p. 41.

4 See Nicholas Stern, *The Economics of Climate Change: The Stern Review*, Cambridge: Cambridge University Press, 2007. The review was commissioned by the UK government and did its best to make green technology appear to be a sound commercial investment.

5 Standard and Poor's explained their assessment as follows on their website: 'Because the U.S. has, relative to its "AAA" peers, what we consider to be very large budget deficits and rising government indebtedness and the path to addressing these is not clear to us, we have revised our outlook on the long-term rating to negative from stable' (Standard and Poor's, '"AAA/A-+" rating on United states of America affirmed; outlook revised to negative', 18 April 2011, http://www.standardandpoors.com/ratings/articles/en/us/?assetID=1245302886884 (accessed 30 April 2001)).

6 Gilles Deleuze and Félix Guattari, *Anti-Oedipus: Capitalism and Schizophrenia*, trans. Robert Hurley, Mark Seem and Helen R. Lane, London: Athlone, [1972] 1980. Not everyone thinks such an addiction is a bad thing, however; there is a website called 'Addicted to Profits' which sets out to feed this instead, supplying tips on how to make money out of credit crises and market collapses (see Dave Skarica, 'Addicted to Profits', http://addictedtoprofits.net/ (accessed 13 October 2011)).

7 See Slavoj Žižek, *The Sublime Object of Ideology*, London and New York: Verso, 1989; and *Enjoy Your Symptom!: Jacques Lacan in Hollywood and Out*, 2nd edn, London and New York: Routledge, [2001] 2008.

8 Stuart Sim, *The Carbon Footprint Wars: What Might Happen If We Retreat From Globalization?*, Edinburgh: Edinburgh University Press, 2009; and *The End of Modernity: What the Financial and Environmental Crisis Is Really Telling Us*, Edinburgh: Edinburgh University Press, 2010.

Notes to Chapter 2

1 See 'Border agency "put profit first"', AolNews, 16 February 2011, http://news.aol.co.uk/main-news/story/border-agency-put-profit-first/1592666/ (accessed 16 February 2011).

2 See Slavoj Žižek, *The Sublime Object of Ideology*, London and New York: Verso, 1989.

3 David Harvey, *A Brief History of Neoliberalism*, Oxford: Oxford University Press, 2005, p. 2.

4 Ibid. p. 2.

5 The remark was made by Mandelson to an audience of business executives in 1998, and widely reported in the media at the time. When *The Guardian* repeated it in an editorial leader in 2008, Mandelson complained that he had not been properly quoted, and that his full comment was, 'we are intensely relaxed about people becoming filthy rich, as long as they pay their taxes' (see 'Money follows power', Leader, *The Guardian*, 11 January 2008, http://www.guardian.co.uk/commentisfree/2008/jan/11/leadersandreply.mainsection1 (accessed 9 November 2011)); Mandelson's reply appeared in the paper's letter column on 12 January 2008, http://www.guardian.co.uk/politics/2008/jan/12/tonyblair.labour (accessed 9 November 2011). Nevertheless, the clear signal

Mandelson was giving was that neoliberalism was being given the go-ahead by an ostensibly socialist government.

6 Jean-François Lyotard, *Libidinal Economy*, trans. Iain Hamilton Grant, London: Athlone, [1974] 1993, p. 111.

7 See Public Citizen, 'Water privatization fiascos: broken promises and social turmoil', http://www.philadelphia.edu.jo/Books/Variety%20of%20Topics/Water%20Privatization%20Fiascos.pdf (accessed 9 June 2011). (Public Citizen describes itself as 'a non-profit research, lobbying and litigation organization based in Washington. D.C.', acting as 'advocates for consumer protection and for government and corporate accountability' (ibid.).)

8 See Jean-Paul Sartre, *Being and Nothingness: An Essay on Phenomenological Ontology*, trans. Hazel E. Barnes, London: Methuen, [1943] 1958.

9 H. R. Kedward, *Occupied France: Collaboration and Resistance 1940–1944*, Oxford: Basil Blackwell, 1985, pp. 9, 45.

10 Žižek, *Sublime Object*, p. 29.

11 Ibid. p. 29.

12 See Peter Sloterdijk, *Critique of Cynical Reason*, trans. Michael Eldred, London: Verso, [1983] 1988.

13 As I have pointed out elsewhere, Žižek's concept of fetishisation very effectively undermines the Marxist concept of false consciousness: the belief that the population of capitalist countries is programmed by the authorities (the theory of hegemony) to go along with a system which is diametrically opposed to their best interests. Much of Marxist thought hangs on this notion, which denies that anyone except a member of the exploiting capitalist class could ever freely support a capitalist economy (see my *Post-Marxism: An Intellectual History*, London and New York: Routledge, 2000).

14 Slavoj Žižek, *Enjoy Your Symptom!: Jacques Lacan in Hollywood and Out*, 2nd edn, London and New York: Routledge, [2001] 2008, p. x.

15 Ibid. p. x.

16 James Murdoch, 'The absence of trust', 2009 Edinburgh International Television Festival MacTaggart Lecture, 28 August 2009, http://www.guardian.co.uk/media/2009/aug/28/james-murdoch-bbc-mactaggart-edinburgh-tv-festival (accessed 2 April 2011).

17 Ibid.

18 Niall Ferguson, *Civilization: The West and the Rest*, London: Allen Lane, 2011.

19 NPR's annual budget is $180 million, and in no way can it be compared to public national channels on the European, or even Canadian or Australian, model. It presents no threat at all to the commercial system that dominates in American broadcasting. Although NPR was government-funded in its early days, only a small percentage of its funding now comes from that source, the bulk of it coming from public pledges (regular appeals being made for these on-air, which can become very irritating to listeners), private grants, and sponsorship.

20 Murdoch, 'Absence of trust'.

21 Milton Friedman, 'The social responsibility of business is to increase its profits', *The New York Times Magazine*, 13 September 1970, http://www-rohan.sdsu.edu/faculty/dunnweb/rprnts.friedman.html (accessed 4 May 2011).

22 See Philip Augar, *Chasing Alpha: How Reckless Growth and Unchecked Ambition Ruined the City's Golden Decade*, London: Bodley Head, 2009.

23 The governor of the Bank of England, Mervyn King, for example, who under questioning by a Treasury select committee in 2011, conceded that, '[t]he research makes it clear that the impact of these crises lasts for many years. It is not like an ordinary recession, where you lose output and get it back quickly. We may not get the lost output back for very many years, if ever' (quoted in Philip Inman, 'Bank governor says spending cuts are the City's fault', *The Guardian*, 2 March 2011, p. 1).

24 Gilles Deleuze and Félix Guattari, *Anti-Oedipus: Capitalism and Schizophrenia*, trans. Robert Hurley, Mark Seem and Helen R. Lane, London: Athlone, [1972] 1980, p. 2.

25 Charles R. Morris, *The Trillion Dollar Meltdown: Easy Money, High Rollers, and the Great Credit Crash*, New York: PublicAffairs, 2008; and *The Two Trillion Dollar Meltdown: Easy Money, High Rollers, and the Great Credit Crash*, New York: PublicAffairs, 2008, p. xiv.

26 See Richard Wachman, 'Dutch bankers' bonuses axed by people power', *The Observer*, 27 March 2011, p. 46.

27 See Jean-François Lyotard, *The Postmodern Condition: A Report on Knowledge*, trans. Geoff Bennington and Brian Massumi, Manchester: Manchester University Press, [1979] 1984.

28 Douglas Rushkoff, *Life Inc.: How the World Became a Corporation, and How to Take it Back*, London: Bodley Head, 2009, p. 22.

29 Ibid. p. 233.

30 Ibid. pp. 234, 235, 238.

31 Institute of Islamic Banking, 'Islamic Banking', http://www.islamic-banking.com/what_is_ibanking.aspx (accessed 19 June 2011).

32 Gethin Chamberlain, 'Inside the iSweat shops: Apple factories accused of exploiting Chinese workers', *The Observer*, 1 May 2011, p. 5.

33 Ibid. p. 5.

34 I discuss the case for this practice in chapter 9, 'Coaching and the Whistleblowing Dilemma', of Angélique du Toit and Stuart Sim, *Rethinking Coaching: Critical Theory and the Economic Crisis*, Basingstoke: Palgrave, 2010.

35 Alfie Kohn, quoted in Nic Fleming, 'The bonus myth', *New Scientist*, 9 April 2011, pp. 40–3 (p. 40).

Notes to Chapter 3

1 'Oxfam annual report & accounts 2009/10', http://www.oxfam.org.uk/resources/downloads/reports/report_accounts09_10.pdf (accessed 5 June 2011).

2 Andrew Adair, quoted in Daniel Boffey, 'Charity shops fear for their survival as councils levy fee on recycling banks', *The Observer*, 29 May 2011, p. 3.

3 For a sympathetic account of American-style consumer-driven religious belief and its international influence, see John Micklethwait and Adrian Wooldridge, *God Is Back: How the Global Rise of Faith Is Changing the World*, London: Penguin, 2010.

4 See 'Funding the Church of England', http://www.churchof englandorg/about-us/facts-stats/funding.aspx (accessed 4 June 2011).

5 The concept of the body as property, and our labour as something to be sold on the market (preferably to the highest bidder), is generally traced back to the work of John Locke (see his *Second Treatise*, in *Two Treatises of Government*, ed. Peter Laslett, Cambridge: Cambridge University Press, [1690] 1960.

6 Janet Radcliffe Richards, *The Sceptical Feminist: A Philosophical Enquiry*, London: Routledge, 1980.

7 A sidelight to this point is that as I write (February 2011) the British tabloid press is conducting a campaign against the higher-paid managerial staff in the public sector, even though their wages, which are admittedly far higher than those working under them, are in most cases only a fraction of what bankers are being awarded in annual bonuses – never mind their actual salary. The impression left by such coverage is that it is having to meet such wages that is the reason for the lack of funding in the public sector, rather than reduced government spending to bring down the deficit created by bailing out the bankers. Yet again, there seems to be one law for reporting on the public sector, and another one altogether for the private.

Notes to Chapter 4

1 John Parrington, 'Universities need proper public funding, not US-style privatisation', *The Guardian*, 7 April 2011, p. 37.

2 For Milton Friedman's socio-economic theories, see his *Capitalism and Freedom*, 2nd edn, Chicago and London: University of Chicago Press, [1962] 1982.

3 Institute of Islamic Banking, 'Islamic Banking', http://www.islamic-banking.com/what_is_ibanking.aspx (accessed 19 June 2011).

4 Ibid.

5 Ibid.

6 See particularly Book II, 'The Ancient Monk', of Thomas Carlyle, *Past and Present*, ed. Richard D. Altick, New York: New York University Press, [1843] 1977.

7 See Thomas Carlyle, *Signs of the Times* [1829], in *A Carlyle Reader*, ed. G. B. Tennyson, Cambridge: Cambridge University Press, 1984, pp. 31–54.

8 The ultimately catastrophic effect of progressive global temperature rises is strikingly captured in Mark Lynas's *Six Degrees: Our Future on a Hotter Planet*, London: HarperCollins, 2007.

9 See Pierre-Joseph Proudhon, *What is Property?: An Inquiry into the Principle and Right of Government*, trans. Benjamin R. Tucker, London: William Reeves, [1840] n.d., pp. I, 38, II, 251. Marx was a particularly

bitter critic of Proudhon, and Proudhon was dismissive of communism, but semantic quibbles aside there is not all that much difference between their respective positions. Both thinkers are clearly very critical of contemporary class relations and the inequalities they are structured upon.

10 I explore this in my *Post-Marxism: An Intellectual History*, London and New York: Routledge, 2000.

Notes to Chapter 5

1 Geoffrey A. Moore, *Dealing With Darwin: How Great Companies Innovate at Every Stage of Evolution*, London: Penguin, 2005, p. xxi.

2 See Thomas Hobbes, *Leviathan, or The Matter, Forme, and Power of a Commonwealth Ecclesiasticall and Civill*, ed. Richard Tuck, Cambridge: Cambridge University Press [1651], 1991.

3 Richard Dawkins, *The Selfish Gene*, 3rd edn, Oxford: Oxford University Press, [1976] 2006, pp. vii, ix.

4 Ibid. pp. ix, x. Stephen Jay Gould strongly disagrees with Dawkins over the issue of gene agency, arguing that he is guilty of 'extreme gene selectionism' in his theory (Stephen Jay Gould, *The Structure of Evolutionary Theory*, Cambridge, MA and London: Harvard University Press, 2002, p. 72). Another to be highly critical of Dawkins on the issue of gene agency is Mary Midgeley; see her *The Solitary Self: Darwin and the Selfish Gene*, Durham: Acumen, 2010.

5 Dawkins, *Selfish Gene*, p. viii.

6 Ibid. pp. 200–1.

7 Ibid. p. xiv.

8 Ibid. p. 166.

9 See, for example, Bob Hodge, Gabriela Coronado, Fernanda Duarte and Greg Teal, *Chaos Theory and the Larrikin Principle: Working with Organisations in a Neo-Liberal World*, Copenhagen: Copenhagen Business School Press, 2010.

10 Richard Wilkinson and Kate Pickett, *The Spirit Level: Why More Equal Societies Almost Always Do Better*, London: Allen Lane, 2009.

11 See Gilles Deleuze and Félix Guattari, *A Thousand Plateaus: Capitalism and Schizophrenia*, trans. Brian Massumi, London: Athlone, [1980] 1988.

12 Dawkins, *Selfish Gene*, p. 3.

13 Ibid. p. 3.

14 Matt Grist, 'Changing the subject: how new ways of thinking about human behaviour might change politics, policy and practice', RSA Projects, http://www.thersa.org/projects/reports/changing-the-subject, p. 4 (accessed 19 April 2011).

15 RSA Projects, 'Social Brain', http://www.thersa.org/projects/social-brain (accessed 19 April 2011).

16 Ibid.

17 Grist, 'Changing the subject', p. 6.

18 Ibid. p. 6.

19 Giddens outlined the Third Way in *Beyond Left and Right – The Future of Radical Politics*, Cambridge: Polity Press, 1994.

20 Grist, 'Changing the subject', p. 20.

21 See, for example, *The Guardian* editorial, 'In the waiting room', 21 April, 2011, p. 40.

22 Giddens, *Beyond Left and Right*, p. 252.

23 This is a theme I develop in detail in my *Empires of Belief: Why We Need More Doubt and Scepticism in the Twenty-First Century*, Edinburgh: Edinburgh University Press, 2006.

24 Grist, 'Changing the subject', p. 32.

25 Ibid. p. 33.

26 Ibid. p. 34.

27 Ibid. p. 44.

28 Ibid. p. 37.

29 Ibid. p. 73.

30 Ibid. p. 80.

31 David Brooks, *The Social Animal: A Story of How Success Happens*, London: Short Books, 2011.

32 Stuart Jeffries, 'What's the big idea?', *The Guardian*, G2 section, 19 May 2011, pp. 4–7 (p. 7).

Notes to Chapter 6

1 Susan George, *Whose Crisis, Whose Future?: Towards a Greener, Fairer, Richer World*, Cambridge and Malden, MA: Polity Press, 2010, p. 4.

2 John Lanchester, *Whoops!: Why Everyone Owes Everyone and No One Can Pay*, London, Penguin, 2010, p. 3.

3 See John Harris, 'From John Lewis to workers' co-ops: these Tories love wrongfooting the left', *The Guardian*, 19 April 2011, p. 27.

4 See, for example, Adam Smith, *An Inquiry into the Nature and Causes of the Wealth of Nations*, I–II, ed. R. H. Campbell, A. S. Skinner and W. B. Todd, Oxford: Clarendon Press, [1776] 1976; Friedrich A. von Hayek, *The Road to Serfdom*, London: Routledge and Kegan Paul, [1944] 1976; Milton Friedman, *Capitalism and Freedom*, 2nd edn, Chicago and London: University of Chicago Press, [1962] 1982; John Maynard Keynes, *The General Theory of Employment, Interest and Money* [1936], in *The Collected Writings of John Maynard Keynes*, vol. VII, London and Basingstoke: Macmillan, 1973.

5 See, for example, David Harvey, *A Brief History of Neoliberalism*, Oxford: Oxford University Press, 2005, and *The Enigma of Capital: And the Crises of Capitalism*, London: Profile, 2010; John Gray, *False Dawn: The Delusions of Global Capitalism*, 2nd edn, London: Granta, 1999; John Holloway, *Crack Capitalism*, London and New York: Pluto, 2010; Naomi Klein, *No Logo*, London: Flamingo, 2001; Joseph Stiglitz, *Globalization and its Discontents*, London: Penguin, 2002, and *Making Globalization Work*, London: Allen Lane, 2006; Karl Marx, *Capital*, I–III, trans. Ben Fowkes, Harmondsworth: Penguin, [1867, 1885, 1894] 1976, 1978, 1981.

6 See Serge Latouche, *Farewell to Growth*, trans. David Macey, Cambridge and Malden, MA: Polity Press, [2007] 2009.

7 Charles R. Morris, *The Trillion Dollar Meltdown: Easy Money, High Rollers, and the Great Credit Crash*, New York: PublicAffairs, 2008, p. 19.

8 Smith, *Wealth of Nations*, I, p. 456.

9 George, *Whose Crisis*, p. 7.

10 Adam Smith, *The Theory of Moral Sentiments*, ed. Ryan Patrick Hanley, London: Penguin, [1759] 2010, p. 73.

11 Ibid. p. 13.

12 Hayek, *Road to Serfdom*, p. 20.

13 Ibid. p. viii.

14 Ibid. p. 27.

15 Ibid. p. 51.

16 Ibid. pp. 177–8.

17 Friedman, *Capitalism and Freedom*, p. 8.

18 Milton Friedman, 'The social responsibility of business is to increase its profits', *The New York Times Magazine*, 13 September 1970, http://www-rohan.sdsu.edu/faculty/dunnweb/rprnts.friedman.html (accessed 4 May 2011).

19 Ibid.

20 Friedman, *Capitalism and Freedom*, p. 133.

21 Friedman, 'Social responsibility of business'.

22 Ibid.

23 Ibid.

24 Harvey, *Brief History*, p. 3.

25 Ibid. p. 38.

26 Ibid. p. 71.

27 Ulrich Beck, *Risk Society: Towards a New Modernity*, trans. Mark Ritter, London: Sage, [1986] 1992, p. 132; original emphasis.

28 Harvey, *Brief History*, p. 69.

29 Ibid. pp. 152–3.

30 The Waterways Minister, Richard Benyon, in a statement made to the House of Commons on 21 June 2010, on the future of Britain's inland waterway system (see IWAC Position Paper, 'British Waterways: the proposed move into the third sector', nabo.org.uk/files/IWACpositiononBW_mutualisationPosition_Statement.pdf (accessed 27 April 2011)). Since then the publicly funded British Waterways has been wound up and a charitable trust appointed to run the system in its stead, a move which will involve exploiting the income potential of things like the country's canal network far more than in the past in order to meet the running costs. Established users of the system have already been expressing fears as to what effect this new profit-consciousness might have on them.

31 Harvey, *Brief History*, p. 152.

32 Harvey, *Enigma of Capital*, p. 39.

33 Ibid. p. 215.

34 Ibid. p. 221.

35 Ibid. p. 260.

36 Ibid. p. 217.

37 Holloway, *Crack Capitalism*, p. 8.

38 Ibid. p. 24.

39 See, for example, Geraint Anderson, *Cityboy: Beer and Loathing in the Square Mile*, London: Headline, 2008.

40 Raj Patel, *The Value of Nothing; How to Reshape Market Society and Redefine Democracy*, London: Portobello, 2009, p. 3.

41 Stiglitz, *Globalization and its Discontents*.

42 Ibid. p. 130.

43 Gray, *False Dawn*, p. 235.

44 Klein, *No Logo*, pp. 445–6.

45 Others to draw attention to the poor production conditions applying in outsourcing contracts in the developing world in recent years include Fred Pearce, *Confessions of an Eco Sinner: Travels to Find Where My Stuff Comes From*, London: Eden Project, 2008, and Rachel Louise Snyder, *Fugitive Denim: A Moving Story of People and Pants in the Borderless World of Global Trade*, New York: W. W. Norton, 2008.

46 Ross Perlin, *Intern Nation: How to Earn Nothing and Learn Little in the Brave New Economy*, London and New York: Verso, 2011, p. x.

47 Latouche, *Farewell to Growth*, p. vii.

48 Ibid. p. 2.

49 Ibid. p. 3.

50 Ibid. p. 6.

51 Quoted in ibid. p. 20.

52 Ibid. p. 42.

53 Ibid. p. 23.

54 Diane Coyle, *The Economics of Enough: How To Run the Economy As If the Future Mattered*, Princeton: Princeton University Press, 2011, p. 10.

55 Ibid. p. 11.

56 See David Malone and Mark Tanner, *The Debt Generation*, York: Level Press, 2010.

57 See Adam Lent, 'Property bubble: could the world be stuck in a new one already?', 14 April 2011, http://projects.rsablogs.org.uk/2011/04/property-bubble-world-stuck/ (accessed 19 April 2011).

Notes to Chapter 7

1 Gwyn Prins and Steve Rayner, 'Time to ditch Kyoto', *Nature*, 449:7165 (2007), pp. 973–5 (p. 973).

2 'Cash-payment has become the sole nexus of man to man', Thomas Carlyle, *Chartism* [1839], in *Selected Essays*, ed. Ian Campbell, London: Everyman, 1972, pp. 165–238 (p. 205).

3 See, for example, Fred Pearce, *The Last Generation: How Nature Will Take Its Revenge for Climate Change*, London: Eden Project, 2006, and Mark Lynas, *Six Degrees: Our Future on a Hotter Planet*, London: HarperCollins, 2007 for detailed analysis of these findings, as well as of the projections as to where global warming will take us environmentally.

4 See, for example, James Lovelock, *The Revenge of Gaia: Earth's Climate Crisis and the Fate of Humanity*, London: Allen Lane, 2007.

5 See also, for example, Lovelock's newspaper article, 'The Earth is about to catch a morbid fever that may last as long as 100,000 years', *The Independent*, 16 January 2006, http://www.independent.co.uk/ opinion/commentators/james-lovelock-the-earth-is-about-to-catch-a-morbid-fever-that-may-last-as-long-as-100,000-years-523161.html (accessed 23 June 2011).

6 The line originally taken by such influential commentators as Bjorn Lomborg in his book *Cool It: The Skeptical Environmentalist's Guide to Global Warming*, New York: Knopf, 2007, although he has since changed his views and become far less 'skeptical' about the issue: 'The risks of unchecked global warming are now widely acknowledged' (Bjorn Lomborg (ed.), *Smart Solutions to Climate Change: Comparing Costs and Benefits*, Cambridge: Cambridge University Press, 2010, Introduction, p. 1).

7 Robin McKie, 'Why Channel 4 has got it wrong over climate change', *The Observer*, 4 March 2007, p. 33.

8 'Solana: the world's largest solar plant', http://www.abengoasolar. com/corp/web/en/our_projects/solana/index.html (accessed 31 May 2011).

9 Alok Jha, 'Europe to switch on Saharan solar power by 2015', *The Observer*, New Review section, 27 June 2010, p. 21.

10 Roger Angel, interviewed by Robyn Williams, 'Sunshade in space',

The Science Show, ABC Radio National Australia, 11 November 2006, http.//www.abc.net.au/rn/scienceshow/stories/2006/1785912.htm (accessed 23 June 2011).

11 See Alvia Gaskill, *Global Albedo Enhancement Project*, http://www.glo-bal-warming-geo-engineering.org/1/contents.html (accessed 25 May 2011). Gaskill recommends that we start by covering all of the Sahara, Arabian, and Gobi deserts for a minimum of sixty years; quite apart from the fearsome logistics, such an exercise would be anything but helpful for the development of solar power in these areas.

12 Barbara Stocking, quoted in Damian Carrington and Stefano Valentino, 'British firms leading the rush to buy up Africa in biofuels boom', *The Guardian*, 1 June 2011, pp. 1–2.

13 BBC News Business, 'Shell annual profits double to $18.6 bn', 3 February 2011, http://www.bbc.co.uk/news/business-12348746 (accessed 5 June 2011).

Notes to Chapter 8

1 This is a factor of particular importance in the USA, where it has been estimated that doctors graduate from their degrees carrying somewhere around $200,000 per head in debt. As Jonathan Wolff has remarked, '[t]his is a serious business' which helps to explain why America has a shortage of doctors requiring a regular influx from elsewhere, with, as Wolff goes on to point out, adverse effects 'in some of the world's poorest regions' as the local medical ranks are system-atically depleted there (Jonathan Wolff, 'Why America steals doctors from other countries', *The Guardian*, Education section, 5 April 2011, p. 7; for more on this topic see Devesh Kapur and John McHale, *Give Us Your Best and Brightest: The Global Hunt for Talent and Its Impact on the Developing World*, Washington, DC: Center for Global Development, 2005). The current UK figure has been estimated at *c*.£22,000 per head, but is likely to keep increasing substantially under the current political dispensation.

2 The view of Dr Mark Porter, chairman of the BMA Consultants Committee (see Denis Campbell, 'Why compel hospitals to compete with each other?', *The Guardian*, 7 March 2011, p. 10).

3 See, 'A survey of primary care physicians in eleven countries, 2009: perspectives on care, costs, and experiences', *Health Affairs*, 28:6 (2009), w1171–83.

4 Colin Leys and Stewart Player, *The Plot Against the NHS*, Pontypool: Merlin Press, 2011.

5 See the government White Paper, 'Equity and excellence: liberating the NHS', published by the Department of Health in 2010, http://www.dh.gov.uk/en/Publicationsandstatistics/Publications/PublicationsPolicyAndGuidance/DH_117353 (accessed 7 November 2011).

6 *Sicko*, documentary film, directed by Michael Moore. USA: Dog Eat Dog Films, 2007.

7 Serge Latouche, *Farewell to Growth*, trans. David Macey, Cambridge and Malden, MA: Polity Press, [2007] 2009, p. 19.

8 Raj Patel, *The Value of Nothing: How to Reshape Market Society and Redefine Democracy*, London: Portobello, 2009, p. 75.

9 Guy Adams, 'The brutal truth about America's healthcare', *The Independent*, 15 August 2009, http://www.independent.co.uk/news/world/americas/the-brutal-truth-about-americarsquos-healthcare-1772580.html (accessed 12 May 2011).

10 Ibid.

11 Remote Area Medical, http://www.ramusa.org/about/mission.htm (accessed 12 May 2009).

12 It has been estimated that the average member of the American military only pays about $460 annually for medical coverage which would cost the general public several thousand dollars. Recent attempts to raise this contribution have met with strong opposition from within the military (see Tamara Keith, 'Health care costs new threat to U.S. military', NPR, 14 June 2011, http://www.npr.org/2011/06/07/137009416/u-s-military-has-new-threat-health-care-costs (accessed 14 June 2011)).

13 David M. Cutler, 'The American healthcare system', *Medical Solutions*, http://www.siemens.com/healthcare-magazine, May 2008, pp. 2–6 (accessed 27 May 2011).

14 Ibid. p. 2.

15 Ibid. p. 2.

16 Ibid. p. 3.
17 Ibid. p. 3.
18 Ibid. p. 6.
19 Medicare.gov, https://questions.medicare.gov/app/answers/detail/ a_id/2038/~/what-is-the-difference-between-medicare-and-medicaid %3F (accessed 27 May 2011).
20 'How can we help you?', http://www.bcbs.com/ (accessed 3 June 2011).
21 Department of Health, 'Equity and excellence'.
22 Ibid.
23 Ibid.
24 Ibid.
25 Leys and Player, *Plot Against the NHS*, p. 5.
26 Ibid. p. 9.
27 Tim Evans, the Association's spokesperson, quoted in ibid. p. 1.
28 Ibid. p. 38.
29 See, for example, 'NHSCA Newsletter', December 2010, which is packed with criticisms of the White Paper's proposals. NHSCA also commissioned a report from Stewart Player, entitled 'Reshaping the NHS and its implications for consultants', Banbury: 2010.
30 Leys and Player, *Plot Against the NHS*, p. 129.

Notes to Chapter 9

1 This may in its turn lead to some very contentious choices being made by desperate students in the search for cash. The British press has been remarking for some time now on the rapid spread of lap-dancing clubs throughout the country, with almost all major towns now having such establishments as part of their night-time 'entertainment' scene. The consequent demand for more dancers as the industry expands has led to many women students being drawn into it on a part-time basis, a phenomenon which has even made its way as an issue into the educational press. Thus *The Guardian*'s weekly 'Education' section feature article on the topic entitled 'Flexible working', which quotes the women's officer for the National Union of Students saying that, 'I'm worried that as women find it harder to fund their studies they may feel

forced into this kind of work' (Rowenna Davis, *The Guardian*, Education section, 15 February 2011, pp. 1–2 (p. 2)).

2 Jonathan Wolff, 'Why America steals doctors from poorer countries', *The Guardian*, Education section, 5 April 2011, p. 7.

3 Daniel Boffey, 'Private university company under investigation for deceiving students', *The Guardian*, 16 April 2011, http://www.guardian.co.uk/education/2011/apr/16/private-university-owner-deceiving-students (accessed 20 April 2011).

4 Carl Lygo, quoted in Daniel Boffey, 'Private university company under investigation for deceiving students', guardian.co.uk, 16 April 2011 (accessed 20 April 2011).

5 'Open universities', *The Guardian*, 3 March, 2011, p. 34. It is worth pointing out that philosophy was already the subject of a heavy-handed programme of 'rationalisation' under the Thatcher government, leading to a series of closures of departments or mergers with other institutions (which generally involved job losses, on the spurious pretext of creating 'centres of excellence'). Philosophy was particularly badly hit, and lost its presence in several universities during the period – a presence that has not been regained, and shows little likelihood of being.

6 See Robert Booth, 'It's biology with Dawkins and history with Ferguson. But who can afford the fees?', *The Guardian*, 6 June 2011, p. 3.

7 Ibid. p. 3.

Notes to Chapter 10

1 Americans for the Arts, 'Arts and the private sector: corporate funding', 5 May 2009, http://www.artsusa.org/information_services/research/impact_areas/arts_private_sector/001.asp (accessed 16 June 2011).

2 Dan Brown, *The Da Vinci Code*, London: Transworld, 2003.

3 Daniel H. Pink, *Drive: The Surprising Truth About What Motivates Us*, Edinburgh: Canongate, 2010, pp. 10, 3.

4 Ibid. p. 10.

5 Ibid. p. 9.

6 Ibid. p. 18.

7 Ibid. p. 77.

8 Ibid. p. 133.

9 Niall Ferguson, *Civilization: The West and the Rest*, London: Allen Lane, 2011, p. 2.
10 Jay Conrad Levinson, with Jeannie Levinson and Amy Levinson, *Guerrilla Marketing – Easy and Inexpensive Strategies for Making Big Profits from Your Small Business*, London: Piatkus Books, 2007, p. 49.

Notes to Chapter 11

1 Predictions are always problematical when it comes to such a volatile business environment as the Internet, but as I write (February 2011), Facebook is beginning to cause doubts in some analysts' minds as to its real financial worth. Such worries may well turn out to have been groundless, but it would not be the first time that an Internet 'success story' had failed to live up to the hype surrounding it: we have been here before with the likes of boo.com back in the dot.com bubble of the1990s. Hope seems to spring eternal in investors when it comes to the new technology.
2 See Slavoj Žižek, *Enjoy Your Symptom!: Jacques Lacan in Hollywood and Out*, 2nd edn, London and New York: Routledge, [2001] 2008.
3 Matt Ridley, *The Rational Optimist: How Prosperity Evolves*, London: Fourth Estate, 2010, p. 13.
4 Ibid. p. 21.
5 See, for example, Martin Jacques, *When China Rules the World: The Rise of the Middle Kingdom and the End of the Western World*, London: Allen Lane, 2009.

Bibliography

Adams, Guy, 'The brutal truth about America's healthcare', *The Independent*, 15 August 2009, http://www.independent.co.uk/news/world/americas/the-brutal-truth-about-americarsquos-healthcare-1772580.html (accessed 12 May 2011).

Americans for the Arts, 'Arts and the private sector: corporate funding', 5 May 2009, http://www.artsusa.org/information_services/research/impact_areas/arts_private_sector/001.asp (accessed 16 June 2011).

Anderson, Geraint, *Cityboy: Beer and Loathing in the Square Mile*, London: Headline, 2008.

Angel, Roger, interviewed by Robyn Williams, 'Sunshade in space', *The Science Show*, ABC Radio National Australia, 11 November 2006, http://www.abc.net.au/rn/scienceshow/stories/2006/1785912.htm (accessed 23 June 2011).

Augar, Philip, *Chasing Alpha: How Reckless Growth and Unchecked Ambition Ruined the City's Golden Decade*, London: Bodley Head, 2009.

BBC News Business, 'Shell annual profits double to $18.6 bn', 3 February 2011, http://www.bbc.co.uk/news/business-12348746 (accessed 5 June 2011).

Beck, Ulrich, *Risk Society: Towards a New Modernity*, trans. Mark Ritter, London: Sage, [1986] 1992.

Boffey, Daniel, 'Private university company under investigation for deceiving students', *The Guardian*, 16 April 2011, http://www.guardian.co.uk/education/2011/apr/16/private-university-owner-deceiving-students (accessed 20 April 2011).

Boffey, Daniel, 'Charity shops fear for their survival as councils levy fee on recycling banks', *The Observer*, 29 May 2011, p. 3.

Booth, Robert, 'It's biology with Dawkins and history with Ferguson. But who can afford the fees?', *The Guardian*, 6 June 2011, p. 3.

'Border agency "put profit first"', AolNews, 16 February 2011, http://news.aol.co.uk/main-news/story/border-agency-put-profit-first/1592666/ (accessed 16 February 2011).

British Medical Journal, DOI:10.1136/bmj.d108.

Brooks, David, *The Social Animal: A Story of How Success Happens*, London: Short Books, 2011.

Brown, Dan, *The Da Vinci Code*, London: Transworld, 2003.

Cameron, David, 'Use the profit-motive to fight climate change', *The Observer*, 28 November 2010, p. 41.

Campbell, 'Denis, Why compel hospitals to compete with each other?', *The Guardian*, 7 March 2011, p. 10.

Carlyle, Thomas, *Signs of the Times* [1829], in *A Carlyle Reader*, ed. G. B. Tennyson, Cambridge: Cambridge University Press, 1984, pp. 31–54.

Carlyle, Thomas, *Chartism* [1839], in *Selected Essays*, ed. Ian Campbell, London: Everyman, 1972, pp. 165–238.

Carlyle, Thomas, *Past and Present*, ed. Richard D. Altick, New York: New York University Press, [1843] 1977.

Carrington, Damian, and Stefano Valentino, 'British firms leading the rush to buy up Africa in biofuels boom', *The Guardian*, 1 June 2011, pp. 1–2.

Chamberlain, Gethin, 'Inside the iSweat shops: Apple factories accused of exploiting Chinese workers', *The Observer*, 1 May 2011, p. 5.

Coyle, Diane, *The Economics of Enough: How To Run the Economy As If the Future Mattered*, Princeton: Princeton University Press, 2011.

Cutler, David M., 'The American healthcare system', *Medical Solutions*, http://www.siemens.com/healthcare-magazine, May 2008, pp. 2–6 (accessed 27 May 2011).

Davis, Rowenna, 'Flexible working', *The Guardian*, Education section, 15 February 2011, pp. 1–2.

Dawkins, Richard, *The Selfish Gene*, 3rd edn, Oxford: Oxford University Press, [1976] 2006.

Deleuze, Gilles, and Félix Guattari, *Anti-Oedipus: Capitalism and*

Schizophrenia, trans. Robert Hurley, Mark Seem and Helen R. Lane, London: Athlone, [1972] 1980.

Deleuze, Gilles, and Félix Guattari, *A Thousand Plateaus: Capitalism and Schizophrenia*, trans. Brian Massumi, London: Athlone, [1980] 1988.

Department of Health, 'Equity and excellence: liberating the NHS', 2010, http://www.dh.gov.uk/en/Publicationsandstatistics/Publications/ PublicationsPolicyAndGuidance/DH_117353 (accessed 7 November 2011).

Du Toit, Angélique, and Stuart Sim, *Rethinking Coaching: Critical Theory and the Economic Crisis*, Basingstoke: Palgrave, 2010.

Ferguson, Niall, *Civilization: The West and the Rest*, London: Allen Lane, 2011.

Fleming, Nic, 'The bonus myth', *New Scientist*, 9 April 2011, pp. 40–3.

Friedman, Milton, *Capitalism and Freedom*, 2nd edn, Chicago and London: University of Chicago Press, [1962] 1982.

Friedman, Milton, 'The social responsibility of business is to increase its profits', *The New York Times Magazine*, 13 September 1970, http://www-rohan.sdsu.edu/faculty/dunnweb/rprnts.friedman.html (accessed 4 May 2011).

'Funding the Church of England', http://www.churchofengland.org/ about-us/facts-stats/funding.aspx (accessed 4 June 2011).

Gaskill, Alvia, *Global Albedo Enhancement Project*, http://www.global-warming-geo-engineering.org/1/contents.html (accessed 25 May 2011).

George, Susan, *Whose Crisis, Whose Future?: Towards a Greener, Fairer, Richer World*, Cambridge and Malden, MA: Polity Press, 2010.

Giddens, Anthony, *Beyond Left and Right – The Future of Radical Politics*, Cambridge: Polity Press, 1994.

Golden, Daniel, *The Price of Admission: How America's Ruling Class Buys Its Way Into Elite Colleges – And Who Gets Left Outside the Gates*, 2nd edn, New York: Three Rivers Press, 2007.

Gould, Stephen Jay, *The Structure of Evolutionary Theory*, Cambridge, MA and London: Harvard University Press, 2002.

Gray, John, *False Dawn: The Delusions of Global Capitalism*, 2nd edn, London: Granta, 1999.

Grist, Matt, 'Changing the subject: how new ways of thinking about human behaviour might change politics, policy and practice', RSA

Projects, http://www.thersa.org/projects/reports/changing-the-subject (accessed 19 April 2011).

Harris, John, 'From John Lewis to workers' co-ops: these Tories love wrongfooting the left', *The Guardian*, 19 April 2011, p. 27.

Harvey, David, *A Brief History of Neoliberalism*, Oxford: Oxford University Press, 2005.

Harvey, David, *The Enigma of Capital: And the Crises of Capitalism*, London: Profile, 2010.

Hayek, Friedrich A. von, *The Road to Serfdom*, London: Routledge and Kegan Paul, [1944] 1976.

Hobbes, Thomas, *Leviathan, or The Matter, Forme, and Power of a Commonwealth Ecclesiasticall and Civill*, ed. Richard Tuck, Cambridge: Cambridge University Press, [1651] 1991.

Hodge, Bob, Gabriela Coronado, Fernanda Duarte and Greg Teal, *Chaos Theory and the Larrikin Principle: Working with Organisations in a Neo-Liberal World*, Copenhagen: Copenhagen Business School Press, 2010.

Holloway, John, *Crack Capitalism*, London and New York: Pluto, 2010.

'How can we help you?', http://www.bcbs.com/ (accessed 3 June 2011).

'In the waiting room', Editorial, *The Guardian*, 21 April 2011, p. 40.

Inman Philip, 'Bank governor says spending cuts are the City's fault', *The Guardian*, 2 March 2011, p. 1.

Institute of Islamic Banking, 'Islamic Banking', http://www.islamic-banking.com/what_is_ibanking.aspx (accessed 19 June 2011).

IWAC Position Paper, 'British Waterways: the proposed move into the third sector', nabo.org.uk/files/IWACpositiononBW_mutualisationPosition_Statement.pdf (accessed 27 April 2011).

Jacques, Martin, *When China Rules the World: The Rise of the Middle Kingdom and the End of the Western World*, London: Allen Lane, 2009.

Jeffries, Stuart, 'What's the big idea?', *The Guardian*, G2 section, 19 May 2011, pp. 4–7.

Jha, Alok, 'Europe to switch on Saharan solar power by 2015', *The Observer*, New Review section, 27 June 2010, p. 21.

Kapur, Devesh, and John McHale, *Give Us Your Best and Brightest: The Global Hunt for Talent and Its Impact on the Developing World*, Washington, DC: Center for Global Development, 2005.

Kedward, H. R., *Occupied France: Collaboration and Resistance 1940–1944*, Oxford: Basil Blackwell, 1985.

Keith, Tamara, 'Health care costs new threat to U.S. military', NPR, 14 June 2011, http://www.npr.org/2011/06/07/137009416/u-s-military-has-new-threat-health-care-costs (accessed 14 June 2011).

Keynes, John Maynard, *The General Theory of Employment, Interest and Money* [1936], in *The Collected Writings of John Maynard Keynes*, vol. VII, London and Basingstoke: Macmillan, 1973.

Klein, Naomi, *No Logo*, London: Flamingo, 2001.

Lanchester, John, *Whoops!: Why Everyone Owes Everyone and No One Can Pay*, London: Penguin, 2010.

Latouche, Serge, *Farewell to Growth*, trans. David Macey, Cambridge and Malden, MA: Polity Press, [2007] 2009.

Lent, Adam, 'Property bubble: could the world be stuck in a new one already?', 14 April 2011, http://projects.rsablogs.org.uk/2011/04/property-bubble-world-stuck/ (accessed 19 April 2011).

Levinson, Jay Conrad, with Jeannie Levinson and Amy Levinson, *Guerrilla Marketing – Easy and Inexpensive Strategies for Making Big Profits from Your Small Business*, London: Piatkus, 2007.

Leys, Colin, and Stewart Player, *The Plot Against the NHS*, Pontypool: Merlin Press, 2011.

Locke, John, *Two Treatises of Government*, ed. Peter Laslett, Cambridge: Cambridge University Press, [1690] 1960.

Lomborg, Bjorn, *Cool It: The Skeptical Environmentalist's Guide to Global Warming*, New York: Knopf, 2007.

Lomborg, Bjorn (ed.), *Smart Solutions to Climate Change: Comparing Costs and Benefits*, Cambridge: Cambridge University Press, 2010.

Lovelock, James, 'The Earth is about to catch a morbid fever that may last as long as 100,000 years', *The Independent*, 16 January 2006, http://www.independent.co.uk/opinion/commentators/james-lovelock-the-earth-is-about-to-catch-a-morbid-fever-that-may-last-as-long-as-100,000-years-523161.html (accessed 23 June 2011).

Lovelock, James, *The Revenge of Gaia: Earth's Climate Crisis and the Fate of Humanity*, London: Allen Lane, 2007.

Lynas, Mark, *Six Degrees: Our Future on a Hotter Planet*, London: HarperCollins, 2007.

Lyotard, Jean-François, *Libidinal Economy*, trans. Iain Hamilton Grant, London: Athlone, [1974] 1993.

Lyotard, Jean-François, *The Postmodern Condition: A Report on Knowledge*, trans. Geoff Bennington and Brian Massumi, Manchester: Manchester University Press, [1979] 1984.

McKie, Robin, 'Why Channel 4 has got it wrong over climate change', *The Observer*, 4 March 2007, p. 33.

Malone, David, and Mark Tanner, *The Debt Generation*, York: Level Press, 2010.

Mandelson, Peter, Letter to *The Guardian*, 12 January 2008, http://www.guardian.co.uk/politics/2008/jan/12/tonyblair.labour (accessed 9 November 2011).

Marx, Karl, *Capital*, I–III, trans. Ben Fowkes, Harmondsworth: Penguin, [1867, 1885, 1894] 1976, 1978, 1981.

Medicare.gov, https://questions.medicare.gov/app/answers/detail/a_id/2038/~/what-is-the-difference-between-medicare-and-medicaid%3F (accessed 27 May 2011).

Micklethwait, John, and Adrian Wooldridge, *God Is Back: How the Global Rise of Faith Is Changing the World*, London: Penguin, 2010.

Midgeley, Mary, *The Solitary Self: Darwin and the Selfish Gene*, Durham: Acumen, 2010.

'Money follows power', Leader, *The Guardian*, 11 January 2008, http://www.guardian.co.uk/commentisfree/2008/jan/11/leadersandreply.mainsection1 (accessed 9 November 2011).

Moore, Geoffrey A., *Dealing With Darwin: How Great Companies Innovate at Every Stage of Evolution*, London: Penguin, 2005.

Morris, Charles R., *The Trillion Dollar Meltdown: Easy Money, High Rollers, and the Great Credit Crash*, New York: PublicAffairs, 2008.

Morris, Charles R., *The Two Trillion Dollar Meltdown: Easy Money, High Rollers, and the Great Credit Crash*, New York: PublicAffairs, 2008.

Murdoch, James, 'The absence of trust', 2009 Edinburgh International Television Festival MacTaggart Lecture, 28 August 2009, http://www.guardian.co.uk/media/2009/aug/28/james-murdoch-bbc-mactaggart-edinburgh-tv-festival (accessed 2 April 2011).

NHSCA Newsletter, December 2010.

'Open universities', *The Guardian*, 3 March, 2011, p. 34.

'Oxfam annual report & accounts 2009/10', http://www.oxfam.org.uk/resources/downloads/reports/report_accounts09_10.pdf (accessed 5 June 2011).

Parrington, John, 'Universities need proper public funding, not US-style privatisation', *The Guardian*, 7 April 2011, p. 37.

Patel, Raj, *The Value of Nothing: How to Reshape Market Society and Redefine Democracy*, London: Portobello, 2009.

Pearce, Fred, *The Last Generation: How Nature Will Take Its Revenge for Climate Change*, London: Eden Project, 2006.

Pearce, Fred, *Confessions of an Eco Sinner: Travels to Find Where My Stuff Comes From*, London: Eden Project, 2008.

Perlin, Ross, *Intern Nation: How to Earn Nothing and Learn Little in the Brave New Economy*, London and New York: Verso, 2011.

Pink, Daniel H., *Drive: The Surprising Truth About What Motivates Us*, Edinburgh: Canongate, 2010.

Player, Stewart, 'Reshaping the NHS and its implications for consultants', Banbury: NHSCA, 2011.

Prins, Gwyn, and Steve Rayner, 'Time to ditch Kyoto', *Nature*, 449:7165 (2007), pp. 973–5.

Proudhon, Pierre-Joseph, *What is Property?: An Inquiry into the Principle and Right of Government*, vols I–II, trans. Benjamin R. Tucker, London: William Reeves, [1840] n.d.

Public Citizen, 'Water privatization fiascos: broken promises and social turmoil', http://www.philadelphia.edu.jo/Books/Variety%20of%20Topics/Water%20Privatization%20Fiascos.pdf (accessed 9 June 2011).

Remote Area Medical, http://www.ramusa.org/about/mission.htm (accessed 12 May 2009).

Richards, Janet Radcliffe, *The Sceptical Feminist: A Philosophical Enquiry*, London: Routledge, 1980.

Ridley, Matt, *The Rational Optimist: How Prosperity Evolves*, London: Fourth Estate, 2010.

RSA Projects, 'Social Brain', http://www.thersa.org/projects/social-brain (accessed 19 April 2011).

Rushkoff, Douglas, *Life Inc.: How the World Became a Corporation, and How to Take It Back*, London: Bodley Head, 2009.

Sartre, Jean-Paul, *Being and Nothingness: An Essay on Phenomenological Ontology*, trans. Hazel E. Barnes, London: Methuen, [1943] 1958.

Sicko, documentary film, directed by Michael Moore. USA: Dog Eat Dog Films, 2007.

Sim, Stuart, *Post-Marxism: An Intellectual History*, London and New York: Routledge, 2000.

Sim, Stuart, *Empires of Belief: Why We Need More Doubt and Scepticism in the Twenty-First Century*, Edinburgh: Edinburgh University Press, 2006.

Sim, Stuart, *The Carbon Footprint Wars: What Might Happen If We Retreat from Globalization?*, Edinburgh: Edinburgh University Press, 2009.

Sim, Stuart, *The End of Modernity: What the Financial and Environmental Crisis is Really Telling Us*, Edinburgh: Edinburgh University Press, 2010.

Skarica, Dave, 'Addicted to Profits', http://addictedtoprofits.net/ (accessed 13 October 2011).

Sloterdijk, Peter, *Critique of Cynical Reason*, trans. Michael Eldred, London: Verso, [1983] 1988.

Smith, Adam, *The Theory of Moral Sentiments*, ed. Ryan Patrick Hanley, London: Penguin, [1759] 2010.

Smith, Adam, *An Inquiry into the Nature and Causes of the Wealth of Nations*, I–II, ed. R. H. Campbell, A. S. Skinner and W. B. Todd, Oxford: Clarendon Press, [1776] 1976.

Snyder, Rachel Louise, *Fugitive Denim: A Moving Story of People and Pants in the Borderless World of Global Trade*, New York: W. W. Norton, 2008.

'Solana: the world's largest solar plant', http://www.abengoasolar.com/corp/web/en/our_projects/solana/index.html (accessed 31 May 2011).

Standard and Poor's, '"AAA/A−+" rating on United states of America affirmed; outlook revised to negative', 18 April 2011, http://www.standardandpoors.com/ratings/articles/en/us/?assetID=1245302886884 (accessed 30 April 2001).

Stern, Nicholas, *The Economics of Climate Change: The Stern Review*, Cambridge: Cambridge University Press, 2007.

Strange, Susan, *Casino Capitalism*, Oxford: Blackwell, 1986.

Stiglitz, Joseph, *Globalization and its Discontents*, London: Penguin, 2002.

Stiglitz, Joseph, *Making Globalization Work*, London: Allen Lane, 2006. 'A survey of primary care physicians in eleven countries, 2009: perspectives on care, costs, and experiences', *Health Affairs*, 28:6 (2009), w1171–83.

Wachman, Richard, 'Dutch bankers' bonuses axed by people power', *The Observer*, 27 March 2011, p. 46.

Wilkinson, Richard, and Kate Pickett, *The Spirit Level: Why More Equal Societies Almost Always Do Better*, London: Allen Lane, 2009.

Wolff, Jonathan, 'Why America steals doctors from poorer countries', *The Guardian*, Education section, 5 April 2011, p. 7.

Žižek, Slavoj, *The Sublime Object of Ideology*, London and New York: Verso, 1989.

Žižek, Slavoj, *Enjoy Your Symptom!: Jacques Lacan in Hollywood and Out*, 2nd edn, London and New York: Routledge, [2001] 2008.

Index

Abengoa Solar, 103–4
Adam Smith Institute, 75
Addicted to Profits, 169n6
albedo enhancement, 105, 180n11
altruism, 4, 25, 26, 55, 56–69 passim,
    79, 103, 148, 156, 160, 161, 162, 164,
    165
Amnesty International, 35
Anglican Church, 39
Apollo Global, 134, 136, 138
Apple, 27–8
Aristotle, 46
Arts Council of England (ACE), 144,
    145

bankers' bonuses, 22, 32, 59, 173n7
BBC, 1, 15, 16, 17, 18, 19, 145
Bechtel Corporation, 11, 31
Beck, Ulrich, 82
Belpomme, Dominique, 91
Benyon, Richard, 177n30
Big Society, 34–5, 68, 69, 81, 91, 164
biofuels, 106
Blue Cross Blue Shield Association,
    117–18
boo.com, 184n1
Boudreaux, Don, 163
BPP University College, 134–5, 138
British Heart Association, 36

British Medical Association (BMA),
    110, 119
Brooks, David, 68
Brown, Dan, 148
Brown, Prime Minister Gordon, 64
Burke, Edmund, 68
Bush, President George W., 21, 81

Cameron, Prime Minister David, 2,
    68, 96, 98
capitalism, 1, 4, 9, 11, 22, 30, 31, 40,
    43, 49, 52, 53, 54, 60, 61, 62, 73, 82,
    84, 86, 87, 91, 98, 99, 112, 120, 166,
    167, 170n13
Carlyle, Thomas, 50, 97
Channel 4, 100
chaos theory, 59
City of London, 64, 86
civil disobedience, 30–1
climate change see global warming
Climategate, 99–100, 107
coalition government (UK), 21, 34, 68,
    72, 77, 84, 110, 122, 133, 146
Cold War, 53
communism, 4, 13, 46, 49, 52–5, 56,
    62, 76, 85, 119, 166, 174n9
compassionate conservatism, 81
complexity theory, 39
Conservative Party (UK), 68

Cookstown Textile Recycling, 36
Corporate Social Responsibility
(CSR), 18, 27, 49, 79, 166
Coyle, Diane, 91–2
credit crisis (2007–8), 3, 5, 6, 14, 17,
20, 39, 48, 49, 61, 67, 70, 71, 73,
82–3, 84, 93, 94, 143, 146, 158, 167,
169n6, 171n23
credit derivatives, 121
Cutler, David M., 116, 121, 123
cynical reason, 13

Darwin, Charles, 56
Davies, Sir Howard, 129
Dawkins, Richard, 56, 57–60, 62, 69,
140, 174n4
de-growth, 73, 90–2
Deleuze, Gilles, 4, 20, 40, 60
Democratic Party (USA), 84
denialism, 96, 99–102
Dickens, Charles, 27
Dow Jones Industrial Average, 25

edge of chaos, 59
Engels, Frederick, 56
Enlightenment, 62
European Union (EU), 39, 93, 104
existentialism, 12

Facebook, 184n1
false consciousness, 13, 20, 170n13
Ferguson, Niall, 16, 140, 152
fetish, 2, 4, 5, 8, 11–14 passim, 20, 88,
90, 92, 94, 96, 99, 107, 112, 156, 158,
162, 167
Fitch Group, 95
FOX TV network, 16
Foxconn (China), 27–8
Friedman, Milton, 15, 18, 27, 45, 64,
72, 77–81, 96, 98, 103, 115, 120, 138

Gaddafi, Colonel Muammar, 129
Gaddafi, Saif el-Islam, 129, 130
Gaia, 51
Gaskill, Alva, 180n11
geoengineering, 105

George, Susan, 70, 74
Giddens, Anthony, 63, 64, 65
global warming, 3, 5, 51, 67, 96–108
passim, 173n8, 179n3, 179n6
globalisation, 1, 9, 19, 22, 28, 49, 52,
61, 74, 87, 88, 146, 157
GOD-TV, 37
Gould, Stephen Jay, 174n4
Gray, John, 73, 87–8
Grayling, A. C., 140–1
Great Depression, 72
Green movement, 3, 4, 30, 49–52
passim, 90, 98, 100, 102–6 passim,
168n4
Guattari, Félix, 4, 20, 40, 60
guerilla advertising, 153

Halliburton, 7
Harvey, David, 8–9, 73, 82–5, 88
Hayek, Friedrich, 72, 75–7
hedge funds, 26
Hobbes, Thomas, 56
Holloway, John, 73, 85–6
Hume, David, 68

Independent Healthcare Association,
122
Industrial Revolution, 97, 159
International Court of Justice (the
Hague), 80
International Monetary Fund (IMF),
10, 11, 31, 39, 54, 78, 80, 87
International Panel on Climate
Change (IPCC), 101
Internet, 18, 88, 100, 113, 159, 184n1
internship, 89
invisible hand, 73–4, 78, 83, 159
Islam, 4, 26, 43, 47, 48–9
Islamic banking, 26, 48–9

Jakes, Bishop T. D., 38

Kapur, Devesh, 180n1
Kedward, H. R., 12
Keynes, John Maynard, 72
King, Mervyn, 171n23

Klein, Naomi, 73, 88–9
Kyoto Protocol (1997), 102

Labour Party (UK), 9, 63–4
Lanchester, John, 70
Latouche, Serge, 73, 90–1, 113
Levinson, Jay Conrad, 153
Leys, Colin, 121–3
liberalism, 77
Libyan Revolution (2011), 129
little narrative, 23
Locke, John, 172n5
Lomborg, Bjorn, 179n6
London School of Economics (LSE), 129
Lovelock, James, 99
Lynas, Mark, 173n8, 179n3
Lyotard, Jean-François, 10, 13, 23

McDonald's, 29
McHale, John, 180n1
McKie, Robin, 100
Mandelson, Peter, 9, 63, 169–70n5
Maoism, 53
market fundamentalism, 1, 71, 87, 163
Marx, Karl, 11, 51, 56, 73, 77, 82, 97, 173n9
Marxism, 9, 10, 24, 52, 54, 55, 56, 60, 82, 85, 170n13
Medicaid, 117
Medicare, 117
Midgeley, Mary, 174n4
modernity, 6, 10, 40, 45, 50, 51, 52, 60, 97, 143
Moore, Michael, 113
Morris, Charles R., 21, 73
Murdoch, James, 1–2, 4, 5, 8, 15–19, 31, 42, 47, 59, 78, 141, 145, 166, 167
mutual societies, 71–2

Nathan's Wastesavers, 36
National Endowment for the Arts (NEA), 144, 145
National Public Radio (NPR), 16, 171n19
National Socialism (Nazis), 13, 76

nationalisation, 11, 63
neoliberalism, 1, 3, 5, 6, 8, 9, 10, 11, 15, 20, 23, 24, 29, 31, 35, 36, 42, 44, 45, 54, 62, 63, 64, 66, 67, 68, 69, 70, 72–95 passim, 98, 102, 110, 111, 116, 119, 120, 122, 123, 124–5, 139, 142, 154, 156, 161, 162–3, 164, 165, 167
neuroscience, 63, 65–9 passim
New College of the Humanities, 140, 160
New Deal, 72
News International, 1
NHS, 24, 109–12, 113, 115, 118–23, 125, 161, 162, 182n29
NHS Consultants' Association (NHSCA), 123, 182n29

Obama, President Barack, 114, 116, 118
Oedipus, 20
Ofcom, 4
outsourcing, 27–8, 134, 160, 178n45
Oxfam, 34, 106

Parrington, John, 141
Patel, Raj, 114
peak oil, 107
Pearce, Fred, 178n45, 179n3
performance-related pay, 31–2, 133, 149
Philadelphia Orchestra, 146–7
Pickett, Kate, 60
Pink, Daniel H., 148–50
Pinker, Steven, 140
Pinochet, General Augusto, 80
Plato, 46
Player, Stewart, 121–3, 182n29
Poe, Edgar Allan, 85
possessive individualism, 45, 83–4
postmodernism, 47, 65, 73, 97
privatisation, 7, 10, 11, 25, 30–1, 109, 111, 121–3, 160, 165
Prosperity Theology, 38
Protestantism, 38
Proudhon, Pierre-Joseph, 52, 174n9
Public Citizen, 11

Reagan, President Ronald, 72, 78, 80, 81
reality television, 17
Red Cross, 34
Remote Area Medical, 114–15, 164
Renaissance, 50
Republican Party (USA), 21, 84
Resistance movement (France), 12
Richards, Janet Radcliffe, 40
Ridley, Matt, 163
Roberts, Oral, 37, 38
Roman Catholic Church, 38
Roosevelt, President Franklin D., 72
Rowling, J. K., 148
Royal Society for the encouragement of the Arts, Manufactures and Commerce (RSA), 44, 56, 62, 148
Rushkoff, Douglas, 25
Russian Revolution (1917), 53, 54
Ryan, Chris, 148

Sartre, Jean-Paul, 12
Scope, 36
Second World War, 12, 53, 76
Shakespeare, William, 43, 141, 142, 152
Shari'ah law, 47, 48, 49
Shell Oil, 107
Sky TV, 15
Slow City, 29
Slow Food, 29
Smith, Adam, 72, 73–5, 77
Snyder, Rachel Louise, 178n45
Social Brain project 5, 44, 56, 62–8 passim, 69, 144, 148, 150, 157, 162, 164

socialism, 8, 18, 23, 24, 45, 58, 61, 62, 64, 75–7, 78, 79, 80–1, 115, 162, 164, 165, 166, 170n5
Socrates, 46
solar power, 48, 103–4, 180n11
Stalin, Joseph, 54, 55
Standard and Poor's Rating Services, 168n5
Star TV, 18
Stern, Nicholas, 3, 168n4
Stiglitz, Joseph, 73, 86–7, 88

televangelism, 33, 36–8
Thatcher, Prime Minister Margaret, 72, 78, 80, 81, 121, 129, 183n5
Third Way politics, 24, 63–5, 67, 155, 166
trade unionism, 67–8
Tricare, 115

US Higher Learning Commission (HLC), 134

Vatican Bank, 39
viral campaigning, 23

wave power, 103
Wellpoint, 118
whistleblowing, 28, 166
Wilkinson, Richard, 60
wind power, 103
Wolff, Jonathan, 127, 180n1
workaholism, 29–30
World Bank, 10, 11, 31, 78, 80, 86–7

Žižek, Slavoj, 4, 8, 11–14, 159, 170n13